Buckaroos
and Mud Pups

Buckaroos and Mud Pups

The Early Days of Ranching
in British Columbia

Ken Mather

VICTORIA • VANCOUVER • CALGARY

Heritage House Publishing Company Ltd.
#108–17665 66A Avenue
Surrey, BC V3S 2A7
www.heritagehouse.ca

Library and Archives Canada Cataloguing in Publication
Mather, Ken, 1947-
    Buckaroos and mud pups: the early days of ranching in B.C. / Ken Mather.

Includes bibliographical references and index.

ISBN-13: 978-1-894974-09-7
ISBN-10: 1-894974-09-3

    1. Ranching—British Columbia—History. 2. Frontier and pioneer life—British
Columbia. I. Title.

SF196.C2M37 2006   971.1'03   C2006-900594-X

Edited by Lesley Cameron
Cover design by Erin Woodward
Interior design and layout by Darlene Nickull
Maps by Ken Mather
Cover photo courtesy of the Historic O'Keefe Ranch

Printed in Canada

Heritage House acknowledges the financial support for its publishing program from
the Government of Canada through the Book Publishing Industry Development
Program (BPIDP), Canada Council for the Arts, and the British Columbia Arts
Council.

CONTENTS

ACKNOWLEDGEMENTS

I thank the following individuals, museums and organizations for their assistance in the preparation of this book: Canada Millennium Partnership Fund, for financial assistance in the initial research stage; The O'Keefe Ranch & Interior Heritage Society; the B.C. Archives, Victoria; Elizabeth Duckworth and the staff of the Kamloops Museum; Randy Manuel and the staff of the Penticton Museum; Ron Candy and the staff of the Greater Vernon Museum and Archives; Wayne Wilson and the staff of the Kelowna Museum; The Nicola Valley Museum Archives Association; The Princeton Museum; and Ken Ellison and Lesley Schweb for proofreading my manuscript.

Thanks especially to my wife, Sandra, for her tolerance of my sometimes obsessive interest in British Columbia history, and to Lesley Cameron, whose final edit of the manuscript has made this a much better book.

INTRODUCTION

Beginnings

The long-horned cattle sniffed the morning air and peered into the dim half-light. They could hear distant, muffled hoofbeats, which grew louder and louder until men on horseback emerged from the mist. As the cattle rose to their feet and tried to retreat from the threat, the mounted herders began to drive them uphill into the woods. Calves bawled and herders shouted as the half-wild cattle were forced from their summer grazing home and headed toward higher ground. Once in the woods, they would be driven into corrals and separated out, some going to market, and the rest released to graze through the winter.

Although this scene could easily have played out yesterday, it took place in the year 1490 in faraway Andalusia in southern Spain. Although cattle had been domesticated for thousands of years, it was here that cattle herders first worked on horseback. The cattle were left virtually untended through the summer in the salt marshes of Andalusia, and by fall they were too wild to be managed effectively by herders on foot. The mounted herdsmen, called *vaqueros*, or "cow herders," were the first in what was to be a long line of men on horseback who tended to the cattle of the rich landowners. They were a rough lot, these *vaqueros*, who lived on the fringes of civilization and were not always viewed favourably by their more conventional neighbours. And yet, many civilized folk regarded them with a certain amount of envy for their carefree existence.

From their origins in southern Spain, the techniques and lifestyle of the *vaquero* spread to the New World, first to the islands of the Caribbean and then to the mainland of Mexico. From there the *vaqueros* travelled to California and up the west coast of America. In the process, the Spanish term *vaquero* became anglicized to "buckaroo." Other Spanish-speaking herdsmen found their way to Texas, where the Spanish influence was altered and adapted through contact with herdsmen from the British Isles and sub-Saharan Africa. The Texans drove thousands of head of cattle northward in the 1860s and 1870s and were given the name "cowboy." The two breeds of mounted riders developed independently on either side of the Rocky Mountains, eventually meeting in the extreme northwest corner of North America. British Columbia became the melting pot where cowboys from east and west came together. Initially, the buckaroo influence predominated, but eventually, in the rugged valleys and bunchgrass ranges of British Columbia, the modern cowboy emerged.

The lives of British Columbia cowboys were little different from those of their predecessors, the *vaqueros*. Hours were long and pay was short; their daily work went uninterrupted by heat, rain or snow; meals, which were often barely palatable, would be gobbled down on the trail; and, at the end of an all-too-long day, bed was most often nothing more than a canvas sack spread on the ground. Women in the early cattle country were few and far between—the ratio of men to women on the frontier was as much as 10:1 in some places. In spite of all of this, the cowboy life captured the imagination of young men around the world. It had an undeniable mystique, which would find its ultimate mythical expression hundreds of years later in Hollywood's depiction of cowboys.

Of course, the story of the cowboys is interwoven with two types of animals: cattle, the source of their income, and horses, their working partners. These animals arrived in the Americas in 1493 with the Spanish explorers and soon made their way through Central America and Mexico. The Dutch, French and English also brought them to the east coast of North America in the early 1600s. Horses proved to be more adaptable than cattle to the climatic extremes of western North America, and they migrated rapidly from Mexico into Texas and California. Some that escaped from the early Spanish ranches thrived in the wild and spread northward up the west coast and onto the Plains. The Aboriginal people, especially on the Plains and in the northwest, quickly recognized their value and either traded for or captured them, then trained them.

By the mid-1700s the Native groups in the interior of what is now British Columbia had horses. Seldom has the introduction of an animal so significantly changed the culture of a people as the horse did the inhabitants of North America. The people's semi-nomadic life, which involved carrying everything on their backs or on dogs and walking to the next food source, was changed forever by the horse. Great distances could be covered on horseback, and, perhaps more significantly, greater amounts of food and material goods could be transported. By the time the early fur traders arrived in New Caledonia, as the interior of British Columbia was then known, the horse was already a fixture and had become a symbol of wealth among Native peoples. The Natives of the interior plateau of British Columbia were the first stock raisers, and over the years they learned the advantage of good pasturage and water for the health of their animals.

The interior plateau of B.C. is well suited for raising horses. It is in the rain shadow of the Cascade Mountains, so it receives less precipitation because warm, moist air from the coast is dropped on the mountains. The resulting hot, dry weather is conducive to the growth of bunchgrasses. All significant bunchgrass rangelands are found in such climates, as the main bunchgrass species— bluebunch wheatgrass (*Agropyron spicatum*), rough fescue (*Festuca scabrella*) and Idaho fescue (*Festuca idahoensis*)—require very dry conditions to flourish. The Native people found that the lush bunchgrass of the interior ranges was especially nutritious for horses, but it was not enough on its own to sustain limitless herds of horses.

Spokane women with beaded bags. Although the horse did not reach the Interior plateau until the mid-1700s, within a century it had taken on significance as a "sacred being" for the Native people.

The size of interior horse herds was limited by two factors. During times of famine, horses were used for food, thereby reducing the herd to only a few head. Herman Francis Reinhart, who passed through the Okanagan Valley to Fort Kamloops in 1858, reported: "We found horses were very high around that part of the country and a good pony was worth from a hundred to $250. Many had died and some had been eaten by the Indians a few years ago when the winter was so long and severe that they had eaten up their provisions and fish laid up, and many Indians had died from the famine. The Hudson Bay Company had to drive in a lot of ponies for them to eat and live on ..."[1]

A second factor that limited herd size was the practice of turning the herds out for the winter without putting up forage for winter feed. A severe winter would devastate the herds and reduce any build-up of numbers from previous good winters.

To the Native people of the interior, horses were more than useful beasts of burden. The social structure of the community came to be based upon horse ownership, and horses eventually functioned like currency. Even though they were a symbol of individual wealth, the animals were also seen as belonging to the entire community, so that in times of scarcity they were shared among the people. This distribution of essential resources was one of the principal roles of the chief. He was the wise leader, the one who made sure that all in his band were cared for, and horses were the community's major resource. Native culture remained centred on horses right up until modern times.

The Hudson's Bay Company

The Native people found a ready market for their horses with the Hudson's Bay Company (HBC), which had been granted a charter in 1670 with exclusive trading rights in the territory traversed by rivers flowing into Hudson Bay. The HBC spread its influence ever westward, and in 1821 the British Parliament extended its monopoly privileges so that it had exclusive rights to trade in New Caledonia. The company needed a large number of horses to pack out the furs it had obtained in trade in the northern interior. Every spring the furs were gathered at Fort Alexandria, located just south of the junction of the Quesnelle and Fraser rivers, for transport to the Columbia River and ultimately to London, in Britain. On the return trip, the horses packed the trade goods in from Fort Okanogan, at the junction of the Okanogan[2] and Columbia rivers, to the distribution point at Fort Alexandria. The brigade trail was used annually from the early 1820s until 1846, when the territory south of the forty-ninth parallel was ceded by Great Britain to the United States. After that, the HBC used a trail running from Fort Hope . on the Lower Fraser over the mountains to present-day Princeton and then north to Fort Kamloops and beyond.

The annual fur brigades left Fort Alexandria in the spring and travelled down to Fort Kamloops, then through the Okanagan Valley and south to Fort Okanogan. As many as 200 to 300 horses were needed for transportation. Every horse carried two "pieces," each weighing about 80 to 90 pounds. The brigades travelled from about nine or ten in the morning and halted for the day at three or four in the afternoon, averaging 15 to 20 miles a day, depending upon the terrain and available feed.

This brigade trail north of the forty-ninth parallel proved to be particularly well suited for travel, because it offered ample grass to feed the horses along the way. Even the rather steep hills bordering Okanagan Lake were interrupted by a series of creeks running into the lake. At the mouths of these creeks were deltas where the bunchgrass grew high, and horses could graze and replenish their energy for the long journey. The HBC traders noted this natural resource and decided to raise their own horses on the bunchgrass ranges of the interior. Horse raising centred predominantly around Fort Kamloops, about halfway along the trail. The bunchgrass ranges in the Grande Prairie (modern-day Westwold) and Lac du Bois areas provided excellent feed and wintering grounds for the growing number of HBC horses.

Under the governorship of George Simpson, the HBC forts in the Department of the Columbia, which included most of modern-day British Columbia, were instructed to take advantage of appropriated land and water resources to raise their own food. Simpson expected the forts of the interior not only to provide their own pork, beef, grain, butter and fish, but also to produce a surplus for export. By the mid-1820s, cattle were being brought into the region and pastured on the lands surrounding key forts. Fort Vancouver, at the mouth of the Columbia, was the first fort to raise cattle. Under John McLoughlin's supervision, in 1825 "3 Bulls, 23 Cows, 5 Heifers, and 9 Steers" were brought in.[3] This herd flourished and numbered 200 head by 1829.

The company also actively farmed north of the forty-ninth parallel. It established Fort Langley on the lower Fraser River in 1827 and within a few years was sending grain, garden seeds and cattle there for propagation. In 1831, Archibald McDonald at Fort Langley wrote that the post had 20 pigs and that the cattle sent from the Columbia River were doing well. In the late 1830s, Fort Langley began producing butter from its own dairy to sell to the Russian fur traders at Sitka.[4]

In its ongoing effort to make each post self-sufficient, the HBC also introduced cattle to the interior of New Caledonia in the 1830s. Fort Kamloops probably had cattle by 1840, and the natural advantages of the country for stockraising would have encouraged the importation of more. Fort Kamloops's strategic location on the brigade trail made it essential that it produce enough to supply the passing fur brigades as well as its own employees. An examination of the fort journals for the 1850s indicates a significant amount of activity in raising cattle and horses. Employees were busy harvesting hay, moving animals from one pasture to another, branding horses and cattle, castrating calves and horses, building stables and killing oxen. The natural increase of the herd was such that by 1859, Fort Kamloops was slaughtering 8 head of cattle every 10 days to supply the needs of passing gold miners.[5]

Compared to the open-range practices of the Spanish-speaking stockmen from the south, the HBC's stockraising methods were labour intensive. Whereas the Spanish stockmen let their cattle roam year-round on the ranges of California, the HBC herders shifted their cattle seasonally in an effort to preserve the grassland ranges. They put up hay to keep their livestock through the winter months and, also unlike the Spanish, practised calf castration and branding. By the 1850s, the HBC at Fort Kamloops was using local Shuswap Natives as herders, drovers, agricultural workers and packers. Their experience in raising horses, their proximity and their willingness to work made them the logical choice to take over the duties of caring for and driving the cattle. The Fort Kamloops journal refers to a man named Auxime, probably a Shuswap, taking over the cattle responsibilities.

This tendency to hire Natives for cattle and horse tending would prove to be one of the unique aspects of ranching in British Columbia. The ranching industry remained an "equal opportunity" employer, judging Natives and Whites alike on their ability to ride and tend cattle rather than on the colour of their skin.

The Shuswap and Okanagan Natives recognized the benefits of raising horses and cattle on their own land and began to acquire their own herds. Their methods of caring for the animals were less labour intensive than those of the HBC. Horses and cattle were left to graze on the abundant bunchgrass, and little time was spent putting up hay for winter forage during the summer hunting and gathering season. The Natives preferred horse raising to cattle raising, for a number of reasons. The HBC was always looking for additional

horses to purchase or hire for its own purposes, thus providing a steady and lucrative market for the Native stockraisers, which expanded when miners and settlers began to arrive in the area. As well, horses were much more likely than cattle to survive a severe winter that required an animal to paw through a crust of snow to get to the dried grasses beneath.

Horses thrived on the excellent bunchgrass ranges of the interior to the point where, despite winter losses, most Native groups could provide every member of the band with a mount for travel. Their equipment revealed the influence of the Spanish packers who worked for the HBC. Lieutenant Mayne of the Royal Engineers came through the Lillooet area in 1858–59 and described how the Natives made their clothing from softly tanned deer hides ornamented with beads and porcupine quills. Most significantly, they also "copied the Spanish wooden saddle for riding and made bridles of simple cord or often of the hair of the wild sheep for it cannot be called wool, plaited. The middle of this is passed through the horse's mouth and hitched around its lower jaw and the ends brought up on each side of his neck."[6]

These early influences would shape the ranching industry in British Columbia. The presence of stock saddles and other horse gear similar to that used by the *vaqueros* far to the south placed the cattlemen of the British

Members of the Lillooet Nation meeting with government officials in 1865. It is significant that almost every member is on horseback, showing the abundance of horses available at the time.

Columbia frontier as direct descendents of the Spanish-speaking herdsmen of the Andalusian salt marshes. Native people were also significantly involved in ranching—something that would characterize the British Columbia cattle business right up to modern times. Much would happen to make the British Columbia experience unique, and by the end of the 1850s the foundations of the cattle industry and the role of the cowboy were firmly established.

Chapter One

THE DROVERS

Approaches from the South

The crack of whips and the bawl of cattle filled the morning air. In a cloud of choking dust, the herd moved slowly out of the frontier town of Oregon City. Weeks of preparation—sorting, inspecting and branding—were behind them as the men on horseback pointed the cattle north. The year was 1858; their destination the gold fields of British Columbia, hundreds of miles to the north through uncharted and hostile territory. They were heading out on what would become the first of many great cattle drives into British Columbia. Over 22,000 head of beef cattle would cross into this newest British colony.

In 1858, the term "cowboy" was not yet in use. Instead, the men, mostly hardy farm boys from Oregon Territory, called themselves "drovers." Many had travelled over the Oregon Trail with their parents in the 1830s and 1840s and now it was their turn to head out on a trail into the wilderness. The excitement of setting out on an adventure was mixed with the genuine fear that they might not make it. Theirs was the first herd to leave Oregon Territory on a journey that promised only danger and uncertainty. Deep rivers had to be crossed, hostile Native people confronted and steep mountain cliffs traversed. And where would it all lead? Few of the men even knew where they were going. All they had was a vague awareness that somewhere north of them, in British territory, lay the Fraser and Thompson rivers. Only Joel Palmer, their leader, knew and they trusted him. They would follow him wherever he led.

Palmer, a grizzled veteran of Indian battles with first-hand experience of the harshness of frontier life, had been born to Quaker parents on Canada's Lake Ontario. After various endeavours in the eastern United States, he travelled the overland trail to the Oregon Country (as the area was then referred to) in 1845. Inspired by the vision of the "manifest destiny" of the

American nation to expand into the Pacific Northwest, he made notes along the way, from which he published an emigrant's guide to the Oregon Trail so that others could come to the "promised land." Palmer's natural ability as a leader of men was soon recognized in Oregon Territory. In 1847, he became the commissary general of an expedition to the Palouse Indian country in southeastern Washington Territory to rescue the women and children who had been captured after the massacre at the Whitman Mission. People subsequently referred to him as "General Palmer," a title that he accepted with great pleasure. Palmer even looked like a general with his powerful commanding figure and deep-set penetrating eyes. In the 1850s, he

Joel Palmer was one of the first to see the potential for the sale of Oregon cattle in the goldfields of British Columbia.

was appointed Superintendent of Indian Affairs for Oregon Territory and, in 1862, was elected to the legislature of the new state of Oregon. In 1870, he was nominated for Republican candidate for governor of Oregon and was only narrowly defeated.

Palmer was fiercely loyal to the territory of Oregon that had become his home. He was determined to see it prosper and become a state in the American Union. But the area lacked markets for the livestock and agricultural produce from the rich river valleys east of the Cascade Mountains. The Willamette, Umpqua and Rogue river valleys had produced abundantly under the settler's plough, and the cattle that had been brought over the Oregon Trail in the 1830s and 1840s had intermixed with Spanish cattle from California and multiplied, but the demand for produce was limited. The California gold rush, which began in 1849, had guaranteed a demand for a steady supply of beef and other agricultural goods, but as the gold fields became mined out and the state of California became more self-sufficient, the demand for Oregon produce dwindled.

In the spring of 1858, western North America turned its attention to the Fraser and Thompson rivers. News of the discovery of gold along those rivers travelled fast and prompted an excitement not seen since the heady days of the 1849 California gold rush. Thousands of miners immediately abandoned the gold fields of California for the fresh prospects of the British Territory. That year saw an estimated 30,000 men arrive on the lower Fraser River. Palmer, although well aware of the transitory nature of gold rushes, saw the potential for a new market for Oregon produce and beef in the newly established

Crown Colony of British Columbia. As the summer of 1858 approached and the flood of men to the regions north of the forty-ninth parallel reached its peak, Palmer began to look for an easy way to bring the surplus agricultural produce of Oregon to British Columbia.

Most travellers to the gold fields came to British Columbia by steamboat from San Francisco or Portland. As long as the search for gold concentrated on the lower Fraser River, cattle could be ferried across the mouth of the Columbia River to Monticello and driven overland to Olympia. From there they were transported by steamer to Whatcome and driven to the Fraser River gold fields. However, the cost of transporting goods and cattle by steamer was prohibitive. And as the summer progressed and miners travelled farther and farther north up the Fraser River in search of gold, the transportation difficulties increased. Travel through the treacherous Fraser Canyon was almost impossible except on foot. The miners had to find an alternate way to the gold fields.

Fortunately, there was a way. The fur traders of the HBC who had travelled through British Columbia for the previous four decades knew of an alternate way to the heart of the gold fields that circumvented the Fraser Canyon. Former Hudson's Bay employee Alexander Caulfield Anderson described this route in his book, *Handbook and Map to the Gold Regions of Frazer's and Thompson's Rivers*, published in May 1858. The alternative trail led through the interior of Washington Territory and joined the former HBC fur brigade trail at the mouth of the Okanogan River on the Columbia. From there it followed the brigade trail through the Okanagan Valley to the Thompson River at Fort Kamloops and then westward to the Fraser River. It had the advantage of being entirely over land and of reaching the Fraser River north of the Fraser Canyon.

Palmer, determined to try this overland route, assembled a party of men and purchased a large supply of provisions that he packed in 13 wagons drawn by ox teams. He also brought along a small herd of cattle, hoping they would survive the arduous journey. The party left Oregon City in July and travelled along the south bank of the Columbia River to Walla Walla. Armed with only Alexander Anderson's map, Palmer began preparations to travel north into the uncharted lands of British Columbia. Only a handful of HBC men who had travelled the brigade trail had ventured into this territory, but Palmer was undeterred.

Unfortunately, in the spring of 1858, a serious problem developed with this overland route to the Fraser River gold fields. The interior of Washington Territory was aflame with Native unrest sparked by the enforcement of treaties negotiated by Governor Stephens of Washington Territory in 1855

Fort Walla Walla. Next to this American military post, established in 1856, the town of Walla Walla burst into being in the rush of 1858.

and the influx of miners to the Colville area. Early in 1858, a coalition of Northwest Natives had defeated a U.S. Army force under Colonel Edward J. Steptoe. That summer the *Oregon Argus* newspaper reported that the Natives "had said that since the fight with Steptoe all the chiefs had met, had a big talk and concluded that the soldiers and Bostons [Americans] should not pass their country, but the French and Hudson Bay men could."[1] It was not an idle threat. During the spring, several small parties were harassed and turned back, and some experienced loss of life. Among the gold seekers preparing to head north to British territory, it was generally concluded that the only safe way to travel through the territory south of the forty-ninth parallel was in a large party organized in semi-military fashion.

The summer of 1858 arrived and the tense situation was somewhat eased by the presence of Major Robert Garnett and his troops in the Okanogan area. Later that summer, Colonel George Wright defeated the combined Native groups in the Spokane area, killing 600 horses in the process. Nonetheless, the volatile situation lasted throughout the summer. Palmer watched with interest as a large contingent of miners under the leadership of David McLoughlin, the mixed-blood son of former chief factor of the Hudson Bay's Columbia District John McLoughlin, left The Dalles in early July and headed north towards British Columbia. David McLoughlin, who was obviously familiar with the route, wrote from The Dalles on June 27 that "this is *the* route to the Coteau country, known as the Frazer [*sic*] River Mines—decidedly so for Northern California and Oregonians."[2]

The McLoughlin party was joined in Walla Walla first by another large party of men travelling up from northern California and later by other, smaller, groups of miners who had been waiting for the situation inland to improve. The combined parties formed a ragtag collection of about 150 frontier adventurers, from seasoned miners and frontiersmen to fresh-faced young men in their teens, all bent on making their fortune in British Columbia. Around half of them had no firearms of any kind. In mid-July the McLoughlin party, with around 400 horses and mules, left Walla Walla. Travelling in military fashion with armed guards in the front and rear, they headed north past Priest Rapids and into the Grande Coulee. The party crossed the Columbia River at Fort Okanogan where local Natives requested compensation for ferrying them across in canoes. Once the party had agreed to pay them in kind, the Natives warned them that there could be trouble ahead for them if they proceeded.

Once safely across the river, McLoughlin's party headed up the brigade trail on the east side of the Okanogan River in military fashion. At one point on the bank of the Okanogan River, a rock cliff extended out and blocked progress, forcing the trail to detour through the narrow canyon of Tunk Creek. As the advance guard proceeded into the canyon, they spotted a Native man on the cliff. He was one of a force of about 200, all armed with HBC rifles, hidden in the cliffs and behind log barriers. A day-long pitched

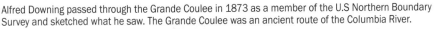

Alfred Downing passed through the Grande Coulee in 1873 as a member of the U.S Northern Boundary Survey and sketched what he saw. The Grande Coulee was an ancient route of the Columbia River.

Sketch of McLoughlin Canyon by Alfred Downing, showing the site of the ambush that gave the canyon its name.

battle ensued. At least three miners were killed and many more wounded. Even more men would have been killed and wounded had the entire party entered the canyon before the ambush was revealed. When nightfall came, the miners constructed rafts and transported their baggage and horses to the west side of the Okanogan River. After more minor skirmishes, and a middle-of-the-night attempt by the Natives to run off the miners' horses, a parley was arranged between McLoughlin and the Native leaders. After some discussion in which the Natives pointed out that the miners had entered their country without approval and were killing their game, they agreed to a treaty that allowed the miners to pass through after paying a tribute of clothing, tobacco and blankets.

This treaty, and the understanding that the Natives required payment in exchange for safe passage, prepared the way for future parties, and subsequent travellers recorded no serious incidents over this trail. McLoughlin and his party proceeded northward, some up the brigade trail through the Okanogan and some branching westward up the Similkameen River. All reached the forks of the Thompson and Fraser rivers successfully. The trip from Walla Walla to the forks took about 30 days.

It is interesting to note that the accounts of the McLoughlin party's trek mention that, on the same night the Natives failed to run off the miners' horses, they succeeded in driving off a band of cattle four miles away. These cattle, belonging to Francis Wolfe from Fort Colville and destined for the Fraser River, were the first cattle on record to travel over this trail.

Word of the trials of the McLoughlin party reached Joel Palmer as he was preparing to leave Walla Walla with his 13 heavily laden wagons and a small herd of cattle. Undeterred, Palmer and his party crossed the Snake River and headed towards the Columbia at Priest Rapids. It was hard going through the sand hills north of the Snake River but after the Grande Coulee, things were easier. Crossing the wide Columbia at the mouth of the Okanogan River with 13 wagons presented a real challenge to the intrepid Palmer, but once again he displayed his characteristic ingenuity. He negotiated with the Native people living there for the use of canoes and, lashing two canoes together side by side, rolled the wagons onto the canoes and paddled them across the Columbia in safety.

Palmer proceeded up the brigade trail through the Okanagan Valley, widening the trail with axe and saw wherever necessary. He and his party eventually reached the Fraser River mines and disposed of their cattle and wagons at a profit. Over the next two years, Palmer made several trips up the trail, choosing pack horses instead of wagons to carry his goods, and driving cattle, or "beeves" as they were referred to at the time, to the mines of the

The "Okanakane Valley" as sketched by Alfred Downing. The spelling of the name of the lake, river and valley was not consistent, explaining why the American and Canadian spellings differ even today.

Cariboo. He never lost an opportunity to tell his fellow Oregonians about the potential markets in British Columbia, and wrote to the editor of the *Oregon Statesman* newspaper in February of 1860: "With a comparatively small outlay in improving the wagon routes between points of steam navigation the cost of transporting supplies would be lessened to such an extent as would give to us much of the carrying trade, thereby securing us an outlet for the products of our valleys. It is evident that if trade continues by way of Victoria and Fraser River, nearly all supplies will be purchased, as they have been, in San Francisco."[3]

His words obviously made an impact on the cattlemen of Oregon and California—the next 10 years were to see a constant flow of cattle northward into British Columbia.

The Cariboo Trail

Thanks to the efforts of men like Joel Palmer, the cattlemen of western Oregon were quick to see the potential for marketing their cattle in the gold fields of British Columbia. The abundant cattle in the Willamette Valley and in the valleys of the Rogue and Umpqua rivers were the descendants of those driven over the Oregon Trail from the Mississippi Basin beginning in 1843. These had come from the American Midwest via Missouri and included a few purebred Shorthorns or Durhams, showing the English-speaking settlers' early attention to improved cattle breeds. This attention to breeding meant that the cattle brought to Oregon were far superior in quality to those of Texan origin. Once in Oregon, they were mixed with California cattle, some of which were of the small Spanish black breed (but not necessarily longhorns).

From the Willamette Valley cattle were either trailed through the mountain passes of the Cascades or loaded on steamboats and transported to The Dalles on the eastern side of the Cascade Mountains. Between the Cascades and the Rocky Mountains were rich grazing lands where the cattle could range freely until it was time to drive them north over what came to be known as the Cariboo Trail—not to be confused with the Cariboo Road, which was constructed between 1862 and 1865.

The two main departure points to reach the British Columbia mines were The Dalles, a steamboat port on the Columbia River, and Walla Walla, built near the site of the abandoned Whitman missionary station and the U.S. military post, Fort Walla Walla. With the influx of miners, drovers and U.S. cavalry, these towns quickly boomed to become rowdy, brawling frontier centres. The Dalles was described as "all that a frontiersman could desire—a regular 'hurrah camp' ... pack trains and quartermaster's wagon trains were preparing to start, some on very long journeys into the heart of hostile, savage country. All was mirth and merriment, no one appearing to care for or fear the dangers that lay across the trail."[4] By 1859, Walla Walla boasted 10 stores, two hotels and a dozen gambling and drinking saloons. The hard-living, hard-drinking attitude of those heading into the unknown was typical of men on the frontier at the time.

From The Dalles there were two possible routes of travel. Drovers could cross the Columbia River and travel by way of Fort Simcoe to Priest Rapids, where they crossed the Columbia again, or they could stay on the west side of the Columbia all the way to the Okanogan River. From Walla Walla, the trail led across the Snake River and north via the Grande Coulee to the Columbia River, which was crossed at the mouth of the Okanogan River. Each route had its advantages. The trail west of the Columbia was rougher going but provided better grass and water, and the one through the Grande Coulee was flat but arid. For the next 400 miles from The Dalles, there were only two outposts where cattle drovers and miners could purchase limited provisions. Those who crossed the Columbia at The Dalles could obtain some supplies at Fort Simcoe, a U.S. military post established in 1856. The HBC post at the mouth of the Okanogan River, Fort Okanogan, also offered limited trade goods until it was moved across the border to the Similkameen in June 1860.

From Fort Okanogan cattle were driven along the old HBC brigade trail on the east side of the Okanogan River. After crossing the border at Osoyoos

Gold-Rush Cattle-Drive Routes 1858–1868

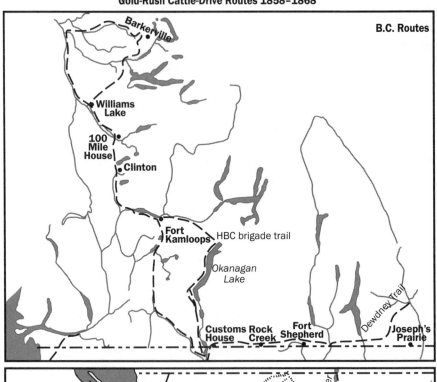

B.C. Routes

Barkerville

Williams Lake

100 Mile House

Clinton

Fort Kamloops — HBC brigade trail

Okanagan Lake

Customs House — Rock Creek — Fort Shepherd — Dewdney Trail — Joseph's Prairie

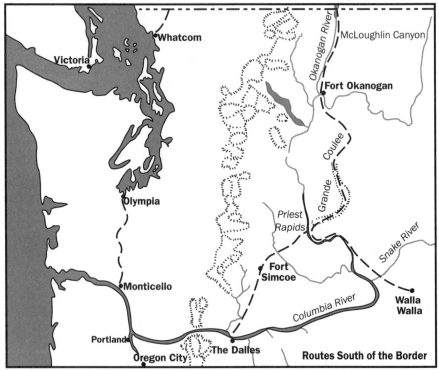

Whatcom

Victoria

Okanogan River — McLoughlin Canyon

Fort Okanogan

Olympia

Coulee

Grande

Priest Rapids

Snake River

Monticello

Fort Simcoe

Walla Walla

Portland

Columbia River

Oregon City — The Dalles

Routes South of the Border

Lake, the brigade trail led along the west side of Okanagan Lake then over the height of land to Fort Kamloops. Staying south of Kamloops Lake, it crossed the Thompson River at the west end of the lake by means of a cable ferry operated by a former HBC employee Francois Saveneau. English-speaking drovers pronounced the ferryman's name "Savona" and the town that grew up at the site of his ferry has kept the same name. Cattle normally swam across the river at this point, while pack horses and men rode the ferry. The trail continued west until it reached the Bonaparte River and then proceeded to the Fraser. Through its entire 800-mile length this route had the great advantage of travelling through rich grasslands, making it possible to keep the cattle in excellent condition as they headed north.

The trail was not without its hazards. Driving the cattle across the Columbia River, especially at Priest Rapids, could be extremely dangerous for cattle and drovers alike. Many drovers lost cattle on these crossings, watching them disappear downstream never to be recovered. As well, for those who stayed on the west side of the Columbia to avoid two river crossings, the precipitous cliffs north of present-day Wenatchee presented an equal potential for disaster. Cattle were lost so frequently on this stretch that the local Natives regularly patrolled the river to pick up the bodies. The same

Francois Saveneau's cable ferry across the Thompson River, photographed by Benjamin Baltzly in 1871. Baltzly was the official photographer for the Geological Survey of Canada's expedition to British Columbia.

difficulty occurred in crossing the cliffs at the south end of Okanagan Lake. Added to these hazards were the almost constant mosquitoes that plagued cattle, horses and drovers alike. Maddened cattle would charge off the trail into the lake or river or, even worse, over a cliff or into a canyon. Other hazards included wolves and poisonous plants, not to mention the extreme heat or pouring rain that made the journey far from easy. Every mile of the trail had its challenges, and the drovers had to be on constant alert to the dangers that surrounded them.

An estimated 500 head of cattle crossed the border at the south end of the Okanagan Valley in 1859, followed by over 22,000 head of cattle in the next 10 years. The colonial government of British Columbia not only recognized the need for food for the ever-growing number of miners and so encouraged the importation of cattle, it also saw the potential for revenue. In 1859, the cash-strapped colonial legislature established a customs duty of a dollar per head on livestock and, that same year, sent William George Cox to Fort Kamloops to intercept livestock and merchandise and charge the appropriate duties. To offset some of the costs of having Cox stationed at Fort Kamloops, the government authorized him to collect any additional moneys necessary to cover his expenses on top of the customs duties. The drovers greeted this rather strange provision with outrage. Joel Palmer wrote: "This mode of assessment gave good grounds to apprehend extortion, for there being no specific amounts designated, and the agent, being ignorant of the number of animals or merchandise to come that way, parties were compelled to submit to whatever sum the avarice of the agent might demand."[5]

When word got out about the tax, drovers tried to avoid the customs agent by using an alternate route to the gold fields up the Similkameen River and through the Nicola Lake country. This route was more difficult as it was extremely rough going and there was less rich grass to feed the cattle. Although this route bypassed Fort Kamloops and joined the main trail at Kamloops Lake a few miles west of the fort, "Judge" Cox was not fooled for long. He soon moved to the head of the Similkameen trail where he intercepted them anyway.

When gold-bearing areas were discovered at Cherry Creek in the North Okanagan and at Rock Creek, just north of the border, it became obvious that the customs agent needed to be right at the border. In 1860, the colonial government ordered Cox to relocate to Lake Osoyoos and construct a customs house there. By late fall of that year, a rough log customs house welcomed the weary drover and relieved him of appropriate sums of money.

Fort Kamloops photographed in the 1860s. The discovery of gold near the fort in the 1850s sparked the gold rush to British Columbia.

That same year, about 1000 head of cattle, some from as far away as California, had crossed the border. Jerome Harper and J.H. Parsons, for example, drove about 600 head from Marysville, California, all the way to the Fort Kamloops area. Each year for the next five years, they travelled to California to obtain cattle and drive them north, eventually becoming the major cattle dealers for the Cariboo. Jerome Harper and his brother, Thaddeus, owned a large ranch in Santa Clara County and were able to take advantage of the surplus of cattle in California and the corresponding low price.

By the spring of 1861, in anticipation of the mining season, there was a great movement of cattle from western Oregon to the east side of the Cascade Mountains. The *Portland Times* reported in early March:

> There are now 1500 head of beeves on the road from the Dalles to the northern mines. C.K. Dawson is here with 6000 dollars from the mines, buying cattle and mules for the upper mining country. There are 150 yoke of cattle on the way from this valley bound for the northern mines. Mr. Thomas has 200 head of beeves on the road for these mines; Murphy and Allen have started from the Clikitat [sic] valley with 300 head of beeves for the mines; Mr. Nott has 180 head of beeves on the Yakima, and 300 head of beeves in Yamhill country, destined for the northern mines.[6]

As the mining frontier of British Columbia advanced northward into the Cariboo region north and east of the Fraser Canyon, miners found coarse gold in quantities unheard of since the great days of the California gold rush. When word reached the outside world of the incredible quantities of gold being mined out of the creeks of the Cariboo, there was a renewed rush of gold seekers to British Columbia. The need for food and other supplies became desperate and the colonial government began to be concerned by the very real potential of widespread starvation. In May 1861, Governor James Douglas wrote to William George Cox, who was now gold commissioner and government agent as well as customs officer:

> The great number of miners now traveling by Fraser's River towards the Cariboo mines will rapidly consume the small stock of food in the country—and great distress must necessarily ensue unless supplies of meat and breadstuffs are brought into the country with dispatch and regularity. It is almost hopeless to expect that food in sufficient quantities to satisfy the multitudes that will this year resort to Cariboo, can be carried into that distant region on mules or horses. The means of transport are clearly insufficient for the large demand that may be anticipated. It would greatly assist in … if herds of sheep and cattle could be driven into the mines. Mr. Cox is therefore instructed to encourage as much as possible the importation

The tiny log Customs House at Lake Osooyos collected duty on more than 10,000 head of cattle from 1860 to 1868.

In 1862, the Clinton Hotel was constructed at the junction of the Lillooet and Cariboo roads. Within a few years a small settlement had grown up around the stopping house.

of sheep and cattle from the Southern Boundary and to be careful not to permit any obstacle to be thrown in the way of persons driving in cattle from the U.S. Territory for the purpose of being sent to Cariboo. Two or three thousand head of live cattle driven into the mines would effectually relieve us for the present year and I expect that number of cattle at least.[7]

Governor Douglas was correct in his assessment of the situation and his expectations of large herds of cattle entering the country. In 1862 alone, 4,343 head of cattle crossed the border at Osoyoos. Competition to control the increasingly lucrative beef market in the Cariboo became heated, with supply and demand causing considerable fluctuation in prices. For those who had the cattle available at the right time, a fortune could be made. The realization that cattle could be wintered just as successfully in the Thompson River area as they could farther south saw enterprising drovers drive their cattle to the Bonaparte and Cache Creek areas and hold them there until the market in the Cariboo was most profitable. Since most of the drovers were not British citizens, they were unable to pre-empt land in British Columbia and were content to turn their cattle loose on the vast bunchgrass ranges of the interior without actually acquiring land. The colonial government, only too willing to encourage the importation of cattle, happily tolerated this situation.

The number of cattle crossing the border at Osoyoos Lake dipped dramatically in 1863, with only about 1,300 head crossing despite a tremendous influx

of miners into the Cariboo. The effect on the beef market at the mines was dramatic. Once again, prices climbed and all available cattle were purchased at a premium. Drovers like Jeffries, Jerome Harper and Ben Snipes, who had made his first drive at the age of 20 and went on to become the Northwest Cattle King, took full advantage of the situation and made excellent profits.

Over the next few years, the flow of cattle across the border continued unabated. In 1864, 3,000 head crossed at Osoyoos Lake; followed by 3,429 head in 1865; and 2,399 head in 1866. However, prices continued to fluctuate at the gold fields. In January 1864, a correspondent from a Victoria newspaper, the *British Colonist,* wrote from Richfield on Williams Creek to inform "enterprising cattle drivers" that not more than "about forty head of cattle" were available for that market and sold for 65 cents a pound. Less than a month later, a large herd of cattle arrived on the creek and the price fell to 50 cents a pound, later dropping to 40 cents.

In order to further encourage drovers, the colonial government began to inspect and improve the trails used to drive cattle to the gold fields. John Carmichael Haynes thoroughly examined the Cariboo Trail through the Okanagan in 1864 and pronounced it to be a "very bad trail, a portion of which is so much cut away by cattle and obstructed by fallen timber, that it is scarcely passable for either herds or pack trains." He reported to the colonial secretary:

John Carmichael Haynes was the customs agent at Osooyos; he later had a large ranch in the area.

[t]he trail leading from this to Kamloops on the west side of Okanagan Lake is the one on which improvements should first be made as it is a road that from its position can be travelled in all seasons—herds of cattle belonging to drovers named White and Cox were to my knowledge driven to Kamloops by this road during the winter of 1861—besides it is the most direct and the least expensive to construct ... I am confident that one good road on the west side of Okanagan Lake would for the present be sufficient for the accommodation of the public.[8]

Opposite page: The narrow trail through the Okanagan Valley allowed cattle to proceed only in single file, and muddy conditions could render the trail virtually impassable.

As a result of the report, the colonial government invested money in improving the trail through the Okanagan, and it continued to be the main thoroughfare during the 1860s. Parts of this trail, worn deep through years of use by the HBC and the drovers, can still be seen today in places like the Garnet Valley and along Westside Road. However, most of it is now under the pavement of Highway 97 and Westside Road.

With the discovery of gold in Wild Horse Creek in the east Kootenays in 1864, the colonial government became concerned that gold and the associated trade would flow to the American towns south of the border. The colonial legislature agreed to spend money to extend the Dewdney Trail, constructed in 1860 from Fort Hope to the Similkameen River, as far as Wild Horse Creek. It also established two new customs houses, one at Fort Shepherd and one at Joseph's Prairie (present-day Cranbrook) to collect duties on livestock and provisions coming in from the south. The completion of the Dewdney Trail in 1865 meant a significant number of cattle were both driven along the new trail and brought over the border from the Colville area directly to the Kootenays.

Gold fever began to wane after 1866, but cattle continued to arrive across the border in large numbers. William Lowe, who was customs agent at Osoyoos, reported: "I am expecting a band of five or six hundred head of cattle to arrive here belonging to Mr. Harper. Mr. Harper forwarded to me a few days ago from Kamloops the sum of one thousand dollars by way of deposit to liquidate the duties on his cattle. It is also reported that a band of cattle is now on its way here from Oregon. These are all the bands of cattle I have any knowledge of being imported at present."[9]

This arrangement between Jerome Harper and the customs agent demonstrates Harper's domination of the Cariboo market. The "Return of Duties for Sooyoos [sic] Lake for 1867" shows that, in that year alone, Harper brought in three large herds of cattle and paid $4,286 in customs duties. Although several smaller herds were brought across the border, only D. Hickenbottom came close to Harper in numbers of cattle and amount of duty paid, with a total of $1,880 in duties.

John and Oliver Jeffries

John and Oliver Jeffries were from Alabama and came to the Pacific Northwest in the 1850s to look for gold. Hearing about the market for cattle in British Columbia due to the gold rush, John Jeffries purchased cattle in Oregon in the fall of 1860 and drove them up the Cariboo Trail to the upper Fraser River. The daily journal kept by the HBC at Fort Kamloops recorded "a large band of cattle arrived from the Dalls [sic]" in charge of "a Mr. Jefferie's" on

October 1, 1860. After holding the cattle in the Bonaparte River area until they were needed, Jeffries was able to sell them all at a reasonable profit. Encouraged by the prospects for the following year, he returned to Oregon to buy another large herd the following spring. In partnership with his brother, Oliver, Jeffries returned to British Columbia. In March of 1861 Judge Cox wrote to Governor Douglas that "a Mr. Jeffries is approaching with 800 head, I understand and will, if possible control the beef market in the upper country."[10]

John Jeffries (pictured) and his brother, Oliver, were among the most successful drovers. They were also fierce supporters of the South in the War Between the States.

During the summer of 1861 John and Oliver Jeffries had driven a herd of cattle as far as Bridge Creek, at the 100 Mile post on the trail from Lillooet. Seeing the advantage of pasturing their cattle on the abundant grasslands in the area before driving them into the Cariboo gold fields, they decided to establish a ranch. In partnership with Thomas Miller, J.E. Johnstone and Reinhardt, the Jeffries brothers took up land at Bridge Creek and, for the next few years, were continually conveying land back and forth between them. They built Bridge Creek House in 1861. Known as "Jeffries Store," the single-storey, squared log structure contained a barroom and kitchen, and a sleeping area in the attic. Bishop Hills, in a diary entry for July 10, 1862, described his visit to Bridge Creek: "At Bridge Creek was a band of cattle driven in from Oregon by the brother of Jeffries. He places at various points droves of cattle. Here one of them keeps a store. Mr. Knipe and I had dinner there today. For a beefsteak and coffee the charge was a dollar and a half. I also bought for my party 10 lbs of beef at 45 cents a lb. We camped about a mile south of the House, and sent our horses across the stream to a bench where was an excellent feed of Bunch grass."[11]

In 1862 the Fort Kamloops journal recorded John Jeffries as having arrived with "upwards of 700 head" of horned cattle.

Like his fellow southerner Jerome Harper, Jeffries was aggressive in his attempt to control the beef market. Perhaps his cleverest attempt at turning away competitors is shown in a letter from John Carmichael Haynes, who had taken over from Cox as the customs agent at Osoyoos Lake, to the Colonial Secretary in August of 1863:

I have been told by a Mr. Murphy who passed this station ... that several cattle dealers having herds for this country were prevented from starting owing to reports circulated by a Mr. Jeffries and other interested persons to the effect that all livestock intended for this country would be stopped on the frontier by officers of the United States Government placed there for that purpose. Mr. Murphy also mentions that he heard Mr. Jeffries state publicly at Walla Walla that I had told him. I have not seen Mr. Jeffries for over a year ... Mr. Harper who entered a drove of cattle on the 20th inst. told me that several stock owners were waiting in the vicinity of Walla Walla to ascertain as to whether they could "get thru or not."[12]

Jeffries was nothing if not clever, for his story had a basis in truth. In late 1862, the United States government, as a Civil War measure, had passed an embargo on all livestock leaving the country. This embargo was never enforced in the Pacific Northwest and in September of 1863 was modified to permit the export of "stock raised in a state or territory bordered on the Pacific Ocean." Nonetheless, the embargo, along with Jeffries' story, discouraged many drovers from heading north and the Jeffries and Harper brothers saw significant profits that year.

The Jeffries and Harper brothers also used Davidson's Lake Valley Ranch and roadhouse, at what was to become the 150 Mile House, to pasture their cattle before driving them into the rugged mountain areas around Quesnelle Forks and later Barkerville.

The Confederate Cattlemen

Brothers Jerome and Thaddeus Harper were from Virginia. They had spent some time in California ranching and seeking gold before they began to drive California cattle to British Columbia, and they were fast friends with fellow Southerners and drovers John and Oliver Jeffries. When the American Civil War erupted in the east in 1861, they became fierce believers in the right of the Confederate States to separate from the Union. Doctor Cheadle and Lord Milton, English aristocrats who travelled through British Columbia in 1863, experienced Jerome Harper's passion first hand. Cheadle's journal entry for September 2, 1863, reads:

> In the afternoon a Mr. Jerome Harper arrived on horseback; he was bringing a drove of 500 cattle from Oregon; a Virginian & staunch supporter of the South. He treated us to a tremendous tirade against the North, whom he called by all the vile names he could think of, hoped every Yankee would leave his bones on Southern soil; South would never be conquered ... Said he was bitter because his mother & family had been driven out of their homes in Virginia where they had nice estates & left penniless. In the evening when we had all turned in he began again a long tirade, in penny-a-lining strain about art of ruling men, intellectual greatness of Southerners; General Lee equal to Napoleon & Wellington ... went on rhodomontading [boasting in a vain exaggerated way] until midnight, wearying everyone.[13]

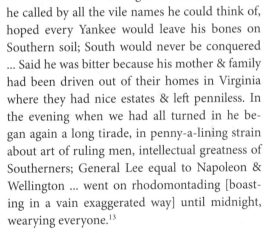

Many of the drovers were American, so the strong feelings caused by the bitter war between the states provoked much heated exchange along the trail. Mostly, though, the strong hand of British justice, embodied in the formidable Judge

The cattle driven into British Columbia over the Cariboo Trail were not longhorns, as is frequently suggested, but a mix of English Shorthorn or Durham and Spanish cattle from California.

Matthew Baillie Begbie, kept a lid on hostilities, and drovers simply avoided those with opposing points of view.

Once the Jeffries brothers had established themselves as major beef suppliers, they preferred to spend their winters in Victoria, living with a large number of Southern sympathizers in the St. Nicholas Hotel on Government Street. During the winter of 1862–63, emotions between the Southerners and Unionists reached a fever pitch, and as the rebel victories mounted during those months, a number of incidents showed just how much the animosity had built up. On one occasion, the American eagle on the coat of arms on the American Consulate in Victoria had a black "stovepipe" hat and pipe painted on it. The next day, a small Confederate flag was flown over one of the shops in downtown Victoria. A determined party of Unionists who marched on the shop was met by 20 or 30 Confederate sympathizers, no doubt including the Jeffries brothers. For a time, until those with a modicum of wisdom on both sides intervened, a pitched battle seemed inevitable.

During this period the Jeffries brothers, Jerome Harper and others hit upon the scheme of fitting out a privateer to prey on American shipping out of San Francisco, especially the treasure ship that left San Francisco twice a month with two to three million dollars in gold destined for the east. The intention was to intercept, rob and burn steamers along the lonely Mexican coast and escape with the treasure. This scheme had advanced to the stage where Jefferson Davis and the Confederate secretary of state, Judah P. Benjamin, signed "letters of marque" effectively authorizing such activities for the Jeffries brothers and their fellow conspirators. They recruited an officer and crew from among the Southerners in Victoria and located a suitable ship.

The conspiracy failed at the last moment when Richard Lovell, who had been masquerading as a Southern sympathizer on behalf of the Union, stole the papers containing all the details. Lovell was discovered and severely beaten by John Jeffries, but the word was out. Thanks to Lovell's information, Allen Francis, the American consul in Victoria was able to defuse the scheme. When *Shurbrick*, a Union steamer carrying four guns, arrived from across Puget Sound and pulled into Esquimalt harbour, the ship was met by Union authorities and all but two officers discharged for suspected disloyalty. The intention had been to take over *Shurbrick* and convert her into a privateer ship under the sponsorship of the Jeffries, the Harpers and their friends, but the scheme was thwarted. The discovery of this conspiracy greatly discouraged the Confederate sympathizers in British Columbia, and aside from a few minor incidents, the war ran its bloody course without involving the colony in any significant way.

Life on the Trail

For the average men and the few women driving cattle into British Columbia, trail life was far from glamorous. The few accounts passed down to us from those early cattle drives paint a picture of hardships and boredom made bearable only by the excitement of travelling through new country.

The drovers would have dressed in a similar fashion to the miners who travelled along the same trail. High leather "Wellington" boots were the order of the day, but the high heel that would later distinguish the cowboy was not yet in evidence. The most popular was a wide-brimmed, high-crowned felt hat, which shielded the wearer's face from the hot sun. Like many of the cowboy's tools and clothes, the hat was of Mexican origin. John B. Stetson would later refine the traditional sombrero-type hat and make it the enduring symbol of the cowboy. Clothing was the typical homespun wool or cotton of the day and the universally worn wool jacket.

Most Native drovers dressed like their White counterparts. Lieutenant Mayne of the Royal Engineers, who travelled through the interior in 1858 and 1859, described the typical dress of the Native drovers: "The majority of Indian parties have now adapted the dress of Europeans and turn out for the journey in trowsers and shirt, usually carrying an old coat of some sort, which they are careful to put on when nearing a town … Shoes they would or could not adapt, although they always carried on their back packs, this was for effect to complete

The end of the trail: cattle arriving at Barkerville. Drovers took up to two and a half months to drive cattle up the 800-mile trail.

the costume. They travelled either barefoot or in moccasins—undecorated by beading or embroidery—in fact a plain piece of buckskin laced about their feet with thongs of the same skin sufficed for moccasins."

Mayne also mentioned that the Natives always slept around a fire in all types of weather and "no matter how cold the night, the Indian invariably strips to sleep and lies with his blanket about him, feet toward the fire."[14]

Supplies were usually packed on horses or mules. A wagon was impractical on the muddy, narrow trails and the chuckwagon did not come into general usage until the cattle drives out of Texas in the 1870s. Food generally consisted of the bare essentials: flour, beans and bacon. There was no awareness of scurvy and drovers seldom packed fresh or dried vegetables or fruit. Some drovers would travel without the benefit of even a pack animal, carrying only a bedroll and a sack of beef jerky for supplies.

Life on the trail could be boring and difficult. The drovers had to put up with extremes in weather, dust raised by the hooves of hundreds of cattle, mosquitoes in clouds and the tedium of endless days of riding. Most drovers preferred to move the cattle at a leisurely pace and let them graze as they travelled, so progress was slow. They would cover about 12 miles in an average day. After the morning "gather" at daybreak, they drove cattle until about noon when they called a halt to allow the drovers to eat and to rest the cattle. In the afternoon, another two or three hours were devoted to grazing along the way before men and cattle bedded down for the night. The journey from The Dalles or Walla Walla to Barkerville was over 800 miles, and the slow progress meant the drives lasted for up to two and a half months.

In most areas the trail was so narrow that the cattle travelled single file, led by an older cow with a bell attached to make her easier to find in the morning "gather." Cattle were frequently lost when crossing rivers, especially the Columbia at Priest Rapids and at the mouth of the Okanagan. Many cattle also died on the steep slopes at the south end of Lake Okanagan. One of the major gold-rush drovers, Ben Snipes, lost several head on this stretch, watching helplessly as his valuable cattle bounced down the slope and landed with a splash in Okanagan Lake. Drovers had not yet learned the necessity of

Ben Snipes started driving cattle to the Cariboo and later became the "Northwest Cattle King."

keeping night watch on the cattle and were content to turn the cattle out to graze at night and gather them up in the morning. Inevitably some cattle would be missing in the morning, and drovers wasted precious hours going out looking for them. It was only in the later years of the trail drives that the concept of taking turns as "night riders" came into widespread acceptance. The drovers much preferred to get a good night's sleep to recover from the trials of the day and to search for cattle in the morning.

Once in the Cariboo, the drovers found themselves in the middle of the British Columbia wilderness where the cost of even the barest necessities was high and accommodation was non-existent. The only option was to turn around and start the long trek home, either retracing their steps or travelling via the Fraser River or the Harrison-Lillooet route to the coast to take a steam boat for Oregon.

Despite the hardships, the drovers' accounts and diaries reflect a genuine delight in the country and the lifestyle. Young men, some away from home for the first time in their lives, found life full of interest and excitement. Andrew Jackson "Jack" Splawn, for example, gives a fascinating account of a cattle drive over the Cariboo Trail in 1861 in his book *Ka-mi-akin, the last hero of the Yakimas*, written in 1898. Splawn was only 16 when Major John Thorpe hired him to help drive cattle to the Cariboo mines. His account of this drive provides a detailed picture of the trials and hardships of a trail drive of the time.

Andrew Jackson "Jack" Splawn's firsthand account of driving cattle into British Columbia in 1861 is vivid and fascinating.

Major Thorpe's outfit, which left The Dalles area in August, consisted of Thorpe, Jack Splawn, another young man named Joe Evans, a mixed-blood named Paul, and the Natives Cultus John, Ken-e-ho and his wife, who remains unnamed in the account. This mix of Native and white drovers was common at the time. The Natives, aside from being excellent horsemen, knew the countryside well and could converse with most of the other Natives whom they encountered along the way. This was especially useful in the early years of cattle drives because the Native people resented, and often actively resisted, the intrusion of white men into their traditional territories—as Jack Splawn and his companions would discover.

Five days out, at present-day Wenatchee, Chief Moses of the Yakimas confronted the Thorpe party, but after speaking with Major Thorpe, he agreed to let them pass. Later that night Chief Moses stood his ground against some of his own people who were swooping down on horseback to murder the drovers and take the cattle. Splawn realized the significance of this act later, recalling, "As I looked at Moses that night, realizing how heavy the odds had been against us, and the unselfishness of his act, I knew that he claimed no reward beyond the friendship one man gives to another. We shook hands and went our separate ways. I would not meet many such men, I knew, even among my own race."[15]

Splawn's party travelled up the west side of the Columbia River to avoid the two difficult crossings but encountered precipitous cliffs where only one cow could pass at a time. He recounts: "Along the shore below us were many canoe loads of Indians, all eager and expectant. They were waiting in the hope that some of the cattle would stumble and fall. The year before, it seems, a band of cattle had passed that way and many had fallen over the bluffs, the Indians getting the carcasses."[16]

Later, just south of the border, some Natives had managed to cut out three steers during the night when Splawn shot at one of them, wounding him fatally. Once again greatly outnumbered, the party was able to escape the wrath of the dead man's avenging people only through the good will of Chief Tonasket of the Okanagans.

The party crossed the border, paid their two dollars a head customs duty to Judge Cox, and then headed up the brigade trail. The names of the sites along the trail reflect the influence the French-speaking fur traders had on naming the landmarks they encountered. About one day past the customs house, the trail branched, the lower trail crossing Rivière aux Serpens (Snake River) and proceeding along Lac du Chien (Dog Lake). A short distance along the upper trail was the "parc" (corral, pen or campsite), and farther on the trail followed the Marron (wild horse) Valley, indicating that, even in the fur traders' day, there were wild horses in the area. Splawn's party took the lower trail, reaching the foot of Okanagan Lake on the third day. Splawn was much impressed by the country around the lake.

This perfect inland sea, ninety miles long and from one to three wide, was good to look upon. Our route lay up the west side through a country that was sometimes mountainous and where, in place, the trail was only a narrow line between the lake and hill. Many small streams flowed into the lake and these were so full of trout that we killed them with rocks in the shallows. I have seen in my day many creeks and lakes accounted excellent fishing ground, but none to compare with these trout streams. The Indians had acres of scaffolding full of trout drying in the sun.[17]

Colonial officials and the Royal Engineers were eagerly exploring and surveying the newly established Colony of British Columbia. On the brigade trail Splawn's party met up with the party of Lieutenant Richard Clement Moody who was commander of the B.C. detachment of the Royal Engineers and lieutenant governor of the colony. Moody was travelling through the Okanagan taking stock of the situation and keeping a watchful eye on the Native people, who were still unhappy with the intrusion of the white miners. As Splawn reported: "The Governor was much taken with us and, to show his good will, sent his page to our camp with a sack of beans and his compliments. The Indians and I danced for joy. Our rations were not over-abundant, and to have food thrust upon us could not be taken calmly."

The excited drovers put the beans on to boil at once and, as they were resting that day, kept them boiling all day. "By suppertime, alas! they had parted with none of their flinty characteristics. We were so disappointed that Ken-e-ho, undaunted, resolved to put in the night cooking the beans. Picture his chagrin in the morning to find them much as they were before cooking at all. He looked at me and said, 'Jack, don't laugh. I have a hungry stomach. Tell me, do you think British beans are different from American?'"

After yet another unsuccessful attempt to soften the beans, the disgruntled drovers decided to bury the beans and pile up a monument of rocks "to the memory of the governor's generosity and good will."

The drovers also experienced the difference between the British and American sides of the border when they reached the vicinity of Fort Kamloops. A drover stood accused of stealing money from another drover named Henry Cock. After a quick trial by his peers, they decided to hang him. As the rope was being prepared for his execution, Donald McLean, former chief factor of the HBC, appeared on the scene and, in no uncertain terms, informed them that this type of rough frontier justice was not allowed in British territory. They reluctantly turned the man loose. Splawn later met Judge Matthew Baillie Begbie, the embodiment of justice in British Columbia, whom he described as "an inexorable man, the only kind which could quell the spirit of the border ruffian."

Major Thorpe combined his herd with that of Henry Cock and the two men drove their cattle along the south side of Kamloops Lake and crossed the Thompson River at Savona's ferry. When the drovers reached the Bonaparte River near Cache Creek they found that they were too late in the season to make a ready sale for their cattle. Most miners from the Cariboo country were heading south for the winter. Unsure about what to do, Thorpe asked the advice of Donald McLean, who had been in the country for 40 years. McLean advised him to winter the cattle at Hat Creek, 20 miles farther on, where the bunchgrass was abundant. Seeing no other alternative, Thorpe agreed and left Jack Splawn and Henry Cock to spend the winter with the cattle, while the rest of the party returned south. Before they left, Splawn and Cock went on to Lillooet to buy winter provisions and there experienced a true taste of a mining town at the end of the season. Splawn recalled in his book: "This town was full of drunken miners, packers, traders and all-around men of the border, all on a prolonged debauch. It was my first experience with reckless, wanton disregard for decency and with the pure cussedness of man. What came under my observation that night and next day was worth more to me than all the temperance and moral lectures I could hear in a lifetime. I had a deep feeling of relief when we packed our horses and bade good-bye to this inferno of the north."

Splawn and Cock spent the winter in the Cache Creek area and were joined by a large number of packers with their horses and mules who also chose the area for a wintering ground. Not far from them, on the Thompson River, was another group of packers wintering their animals. Among them was Lewis Campbell, who would become a very successful drover in the years to come and who would settle in the Kamloops area a few years later.

Despite occasional frigid temperatures, all the cattle survived the winter of 1861–62, feeding on the abundant bunchgrass in the area as well as the sagebrush known as "wormwood." By spring they were in good condition and soon fattened up on the green grass that sprang up. However, the winter in Washington and Oregon had not been so mild. In fact, it had been a devastating winter and thousands of cattle had died from the severe cold. As prices for beef soared in the gold fields because of the resulting shortage of cattle from Oregon and Washington, Thorpe found himself with a herd that was worth a fortune. He was able to drive his cattle 200 miles north into the Cariboo and sell them for up to $150 a head—not a bad price considering the fact that the cattle had been purchased in Oregon for as little as $10 per head. This was the highest amount paid for cattle at any one time in the Cariboo, and even the more moderate going rate of $50 a head represented a fair profit to those with the fortitude to drive their herd over 800 miles of hazardous trail.

Jack Splawn stayed with the Thorpe herd until it reached Lightning Creek in the heart of the Cariboo gold fields. He remained in Quesnelle Mouth (modern-day Quesnel) and there he witnessed a piece of Canadian history in the making.

While in this village, I was surprised to see, one day in September, a large raft, with people on it, floating down the Fraser River. I aroused the inhabitants of the place, who were all in the store and saloon, playing poker. Picking up ropes, they ran to the riverbank. The occupants of the strange craft were pulling toward shore with oars. When near enough, they threw a rope to us and willing hands pulled them in. They were a sorry sight, twenty men, gaunt and almost naked, with four poor oxen, all that was left of a once promising outfit. They were a portion of a party of over a hundred men who left Canada overland for Cariboo via Edmonton ... The present party had kept on the course of the main travelled trail of the HBC to Ft. George, where carts were abandoned and the oxen killed for food. Many had already lost their lives in the long stretch of uninhabited country, and many more had starved or been drowned in the turbulent waters. This handful of men, without means or implements of labor, was the sum total of the expedition. This was pioneering, hewing the way, with blood, for a succeeding generation.

The group of Overlanders, as they were called, that Splawn witnessed arriving were actually about half of those who made it to British Columbia. The other half arrived successfully at Fort Kamloops at about the same time. Some of the Overlanders proceeded to mine for gold on Williams Creek while others chose to go through to Victoria or to take up land and start farming. Many of them stayed on to make British Columbia their home, leaving their mark on the history of the country forever.

After Major Thorpe had spent most of the year disposing of his cattle, he and Splawn returned to Oregon. But Splawn had developed a taste for the adventure and excitement of the trail. In 1863, he returned to the Cariboo with 40 pack animals loaded with bacon. He remained involved in the cattle business for the next 35 years, making his last cattle drive from British Columbia to Washington in 1896.

Another drover who regularly travelled the trail to the Cariboo was Thomas Menefee. He had been a member of the McLoughlin party and had been severely wounded in the battle with the Natives, having been shot several times. Robert Frost, another member of the party, described how his wounds were treated:

We had an Irish sailor in the party (I have forgotten his name) who had been in the English navy, & had been through the Crimean War at Sebastapol. He was the nearest we had to a doctor. Several of the boys were provided with a box of pills. He selected one, & gave each wounded man a dose, then made a clean pointed stick to probe the wounds with, enough to keep them open, & after washing them, laid a piece of wet cloth on the wounds, & would go around twice or more in the day, & probe and wash. The pills, stick, cloth & water did the whole business. They all got well, but it took Menefee the longest to get over it.[18]

Menefee not only survived, he also became one of the first men to enter the Cariboo country as a member of the Dunlevy party that explored the Quesnel River. After two successful years mining for gold in the Cariboo, Menefee and his partner, Dudley Moreland, purchased the Davidson ranch and stopping house near Williams Lake for $15,000 in 1861. Thomas Davidson and Moses Danceralt had established this ranch the previous year, but when the Cariboo Road was surveyed to bypass Williams Lake, they sold it and moved a few miles farther east. From there, Menefee would travel to Oregon to purchase cattle and drive them north. His great love, though, was horse racing, and he purchased several thoroughbred horses in Oregon, which he raced in Barkerville, Williams Lake and the Cornwall Ranch near Cache Creek. Menefee was a true character and lived life to the fullest. One of his partners in the Dunlevy party, Alex McInnis, described him:

A rather slight but wiry build, he was the comic of the outfit, a born entertainer ... song and dance emanated from him "like scent from a woman" as Dunlevy would say, or "'like skunk pee" as Ira Crowe would snap, when Tom's antics exasperated him, but just the same they all liked him. A hat worn at a rakish angle on the back of his head gave him a devil-may-care air that suited him, with his close-set eyes, long lean face, a jutting lower jaw and chin whiskers would at times give him a foxy appearance that also suited him, for he was by nature a foxy fellow.[19]

Another excellent first-hand account of travel over the trail is found in the diaries of Myron Robert Brown, who kept daily records as he travelled the trail.[20] Brown was only a child when his parents travelled over the Oregon Trail in 1852. When their wagon train arrived in Portland, Brown's father died, leaving his wife with Myron, aged six, and his sister, aged four, in a strange land. During their first winter in Oregon, the family existed on potatoes and any wild game they could obtain. However, like true pioneers, the family persisted through their hardships and took up land in the Willamette River Valley south of Oregon City. Mrs. Brown remarried and the family continued farming in the fertile valley. When Myron Brown turned 21 he made three cattle drives up the trail in 1867 and 1868, leaving behind two small pocket diaries with cryptic entries in pencil. Despite the brevity of the daily entries, they reveal a sense of the adventure and daily hardships experienced when driving uncooperative animals up the brigade trail.

Like Major Thorpe's party, Brown's party consisted of a mix of Native and white drovers. Brown's first drive in 1868 consisted of five whites and five Natives, "with all a rather agreeable crowd all things considered," as Brown recorded.

One of the greatest difficulties Brown encountered was the standard problem of cattle wandering off during the night. Brown's diaries make frequent reference to finding cattle missing and having to hunt for them before proceeding. Sometimes most of the morning or even a whole day was lost as they searched for strayed cattle. On Brown's third trip up the trail he was put in charge of the drive, and with the wisdom that comes only through bitter experience, he regularly posted a night guard to keep the cattle from wandering too far.

Other trials also kept the drovers on the alert. Myron Brown described some of the hardships that had to be endured:

Tuesday March 5, 1867—Three of us went up on the mountain to look after cattle. Found one cow down partly eaten by wolves.

Monday June 17, 1867—Passed the customhouse & camped just across the line. The mosquitoes are bad. Had a free fight in camp this morning between Gates & Sharp.

Sunday April 26, 1868—Today we lay by. I spent most of the day in camp reading & singing as usual with George. In the evening William and I went out among the cattle & while out a heavy thunderstorm came up which stampeded the whole band. We then got some horses & went after & stopped them without much trouble.

Monday May 18, 1868—About daylight it commenced to snow and rain, which continued till nearly noon. We found it delightful work gathering up the drove out of the wet brush. Drove 13 miles & camped on a nice rolling prairie. Mailed a letter home.

Friday June 5, 1868—Today we followed the lake [Okanagan] & nooned at the foot of it where I bought $.50 worth of milk & potatoes. After dinner came down & camped near White Lake. Mosquitoes are bad company, which I am compelled to keep though against my will.

Tuesday September 29, 1868—By counting found one missing which I went back & found. On the road one of the largest steers in the band died from poison. Drove about 10 miles & stopped at camp in the woods. Day very cold & smoky.

However, the oddest difficulty encountered on the trail was one that Brown relates as he travelled north from Lake Okanagan toward Fort Kamloops: "Wednesday October 7, 1868: After driving a mile or two, 3 camels came up behind and took possession of the drove, as our horses became unmanageable. I then changed horses and drove them off. We then went on without further molestation and arrived in camp a little below Duck's Lake having come ·12 miles. Day cold and smoky."

The camels were originally imported from the southern United States for use as pack animals on the Cariboo road. Although they were capable of carrying huge loads, their feet were badly cut up on the rocky trails and roads, and they had the added disadvantage of causing terror in any horses they encountered, causing stampedes and runaways. They were pronounced a failure and turned loose in the area where Brown encountered them in 1868.

Life on the trail was not all work. Like any young man, Brown was never too tired to explore the countryside after a hard day's drive. Whenever possible, he went duck hunting or fishing to supplement the meagre rations. Like Splawn, Brown and his party discovered the abundance of fish in the creeks running into Okanagan Lake. He reported in his diary for September 25, 1868: "Started before sunrise. Found all the cattle. Drove about 8 miles,

Camels proved to be unsuccessful as pack animals on the Cariboo Road, and their unfamiliar smell caused havoc among horses and cattle.

passing one rocky point & camped in the brush bottom. Got in by noon. Great excitement in camp! Grand fishing excursion; 60 fish caught in two hours. Splendid fun."

Brown frequently eulogized about the beauty of the countryside. As he waited to cross the Columbia River he noted in his diary "This is a romantic place: high hills, rocks, sand & water all in sight at once & when the wind blows, the sand is the most prominent." Later on, as he travelled up the Okanagan Valley, he would write, "This is a nice place, mountains covered with snow all around & beautiful valley covered with grass & flowers all in sight at once." His favourite spot seems to have been at the head of Lake Okanagan: "Travelled over beautiful country. Reached the head of the lake. Of all I have seen, I love this the best. Tis the land of my choice. Oh here let me rest."

Many of the young men did stay to establish their own ranches in the lush bunchgrass areas of the Okanagan Valley and Thompson and Bonaparte rivers. The cattle that they brought to British Columbia became the foundation herds for the cattle industry in the province. In fact, by 1869, with the market in the Cariboo declining, the local ranches easily supplied the needs of the mining population, and few cattle were brought into British Columbia. While drovers continued to bring cattle into British Columbia, primarily for the new mining centres in the Kootenays, the era of the large-scale cattle drives had passed into history.

Chapter Two

THE RANCHERS

Roadside Ranches

Archibald McKinlay was sore and tired and covered with the dust of a long day's ride when he rode up yet another hill in the B.C. interior on a hot summer day in 1862. He had been on the trail for six weeks, all the way from Oregon City, some 700 miles to the south. But when he crested the hill, his heart leapt. Before him lay a large lake, shimmering in the evening sun and surrounded by lush, rolling hills. This was the spot he remembered from 20 years earlier when he had worked as a labourer for the HBC. On one of his many trips up the brigade trail for the company, his brigade had camped beside this lake. McKinlay had vowed then that some day he would return to settle there. Now, after losing his own little trading post to the flooding of the Willamette River, he was back to stay. He staked out his 160-acre pre-emption alongside the lake adjoining the trail and constructed several ranch buildings before returning to Oregon City for the winter. The next spring, he headed north again with his wife, Sarah, their five children, his mother-in-law and her brother. They arrived at Lac La Hache ("Axe Lake," so named by the French-speaking HBC employees) and set up the 115 Mile House as a ranch and stopping house. The McKinlay family would remain there for the next 70 years.

The gold-rush years changed the landscape forever. Roadside ranches like McKinlay's sprang up all along the Cariboo Road and other routes into the interior. More enterprising drovers settled on land along the road, seizing the opportunity to prosper by supplying food and lodging to the miners, freighters and stagecoaches streaming to the gold fields. Many of them, especially those along the Cariboo Road, established stopping houses to profit from the steady stream of miners and other adventurers on their way to and from the Cariboo.

Teamsters and freight wagons on the Cariboo Road at Bonaparte in 1871. Note the BC Express (BX) stagecoaches; they connected Yale on the lower Fraser River with Barkerville, making it the longest stagecoach line in North America at the time.

William H. Kay's ranch at the 129 Mile post on the Cariboo Road. In spite of their isolation, Mrs. Kay is dressed in her fashionable hoop skirt.

Thomas Roper's 122 Mile Ranch. Like most ranches on the Cariboo Road, Roper's raised beef and dairy cattle, vegetables and chickens, as well as serving as a stopping house for travellers.

The "mile houses," as they were called, were named for the distance they were located from "Mile Zero" at Lillooet, and were scattered along the Cut-off Valley to Clinton and along the Cariboo Wagon Road. The owners produced their own crops and usually kept a herd of cattle to supply fresh beef to their patrons. Many of these names are still with us today, as in 110 Mile House and the 108 Mile Ranch.

Other former drovers, particularly those in the more isolated Thompson, Nicola and Okanagan regions, saw the potential for stockraising on the lush bunchgrass ranges of the interior and were content to set up farms or ranches where they could make a living and await the future development of the country. By 1868, when the gold rush was a mere shadow of its former self, there were a series of ranches "strung like beads along a few roads and trails."[1] Ranchers took advantage of the new Land Ordinance of 1870 to pre-empt 320 acres of land at any one time in the area east of the Cascade Mountains, double the previous allowance. The ordinance also provided for the purchase of an unlimited amount of additional lands at the cost of one dollar per acre, provided that the land had been surveyed. Surveyors began the long and painstaking task of surveying the rugged interior, being careful to honour and include the existing pre-emptions. These original lots were often at variance to the strict grid established by the surveyors, and even today, the first pre-emptions can be spotted easily on survey maps by their odd shapes.

Unfortunately, the dwindling of gold-rush activity meant the market for fresh beef had also dwindled. The 4,628 people living in the Colony of British Columbia in 1871 created a small demand for beef, but most consumers were living along the coast. Those based along the Cariboo Road could sell a certain amount of beef to the freighters and stagecoach customers who travelled the road, but the number of cattle fed on the rich grasses of the interior soon outstripped the market demand. By the early 1870s, cattle were regularly being driven to the coastal markets of New Westminster, Victoria and Nanaimo, but these coastal centres still imported, by ship, over 1,000 head annually. These small markets brought little reward for the long trail drive and discouraged many of those who had settled along the Cariboo Road during the gold-rush years. They simply moved on, either leaving their pre-emption to lapse or selling to neighbouring ranchers.

But change beckoned again. The new Dominion of Canada was negotiating for the colony to unite with it. Confederation promised, among other things, that within two years the Dominion would begin constructing a railway to connect B.C. with the eastern provinces. The terms further stipulated that the railway would be completed within 10 years. Such a promise virtually guaranteed the acceptance of the terms by the people of B.C. Ranchers in the

Thompson, Nicola and Okanagan regions saw the railway as an answer to their dreams. Those with sufficient vision and determination to wait until the eastern markets became available also saw an opportunity to acquire enough land to secure their future once the new railway arrived. Amassing whatever capital they could, many ranchers profited from their less fortunate neighbours' misery and built up their holdings by buying available properties at cheap prices.

Those ranchers investing in the future engaged in mixed farming, cultivating vegetables and crops as well as raising cattle. The ranches along the Cariboo Road also earned a few dollars by maintaining a supply of horses for the stagecoach lines, which needed fresh horses at intervals of about 18 miles. Six horses were required to pull each stagecoach, so a large number of horses had to be maintained along the route. In addition, stagecoach passengers had to be fed and accommodated, thus creating an opportunity for additional income for Cariboo Road's residents.

For most of the day-to-day ranching activities, the ranchers themselves and their families were the workers. They looked after the feeding, seasonal moving of herds and doctoring of sick cattle, but the longer trail drives and the

spring and fall roundups required additional men to assist. In most cases, the need for labour was filled by the local Native bands. Not only were the Native people close at hand and available at short notice, but they were also excellent horsemen and could withstand the harsh conditions of the B.C. interior. The ranchers soon recognized the value of their Native neighbours and their contribution to the ranching economy. In turn, the Native people could earn much-needed money by working in an area that was a natural extension of their traditional lifestyle, living close to the land and working as a team.

Europeans, Americans, Mexicans and sometimes Chinese, who were newly arrived in the province, were also a source of labour. Many of them had initially been attracted to the area by the lure of gold but had seen the difficulties and futility of trying to make a living through mining. These would-be miners included a number of younger sons of well-to-do British families who were in British Columbia to make their fortune in "the colonies."

Native packers in the South Okanagan. The Natives were natural horsemen and succeeded in anything connected with horses.

Most of the immigrants who worked on the ranches in the 1870s did so in order to learn the basics of ranching in the interior and to make enough money to get established on their own land. For this reason they were not a long-term source of labour but could offer their services for a short time.

Lewis Campbell

Lewis Campbell was born in Ohio, to Highland Scottish parents. When he was eight, his family moved to nearby Indiana where a young man named Johnny Wilson came to work for his family. Although different in temperament, the two young men shared a common dream to travel and make their fortunes. It was perhaps inevitable that news of the great gold discoveries in California would prompt them to pack up and make their way, separately, to the Golden State, arriving there in 1853. Campbell located claims in Northern California but the rich gold seemed to elude him, so he worked as a teamster and packer between Maryville and Greka until word reached California of the discovery of gold in British Columbia. He then headed north.

Arriving at Yale along with thousands of other would-be miners, Campbell started placer mining on the sand and gravel bars of the Lower Fraser. He was no luckier there than he had been in California and, once again, he abandoned his shovel and pan for pack horses. As mining excitement spread north up the Fraser, Campbell followed, being among the first to take pack horses up the trail to Lillooet and the Cariboo Country. During the 1860 mining season, Campbell operated a store in Quesnelle Forks as an outlet for the goods he was packing into the Cariboo, but it turned out to be more lucrative to pack in supplies than to be tied up with selling them. For the next three years, he worked as a packer during the summer months and wintered his horses and oxen on the bunchgrass ranges of the Bonaparte River.

By 1864 he had amassed a considerable amount of gold for his efforts. When his old friend Johnny Wilson approached him to travel with him to Oregon and purchase cattle to stock ranches he jumped at the chance. The two men left that fall and, after wintering in Oregon, headed north with a large herd of cattle. They travelled up the cattle trail through the Okanagan Valley and held them on land about 15 miles east of Fort Kamloops on a small creek. A year later, Wilson left to take up land in the Savona area, and Campbell filed a pre-emption on the small creek that came to be, and is still, called Campbell Creek.

During the lean years following the gold rush, Campbell looked to the northern gold fields as an outlet for his cattle and, in April of 1874, drove 125 head north. Four months later he arrived at Dease Lake, just at the height of the Cassiar gold rush, and sold the cattle at a profit, steering him through the difficult times. When the Canadian Pacific Railway (CPR) was completed in

1885 and passed through his ranch, he was assured of success. He eventually amassed a herd of 3000 head of cattle that grazed on his extensive ranges, which ran for close to 25 miles east from Kamloops. In the early days ranches ran their cattle until they were five or six years old and the horns grew quite long. Legend tells that the last of the Campbell cattle could barely clear their horns through a cattle car door and that they were as wild as deer.

Since his ranges extended to the outskirts of Kamloops, there were occasional problems with cattle helping themselves to the townspeople's gardens. The City of Kamloops therefore hired a pound-keeper to impound cattle that were trespassing on town property. Eager to fulfill his contract, the pound-keeper rounded up about 50 head of Campbell cattle that had strayed into the town limits. Campbell proved reluctant to pay the fine for so many head and summoned his eldest son, Walter, who was the cattle foreman for the ranch and acknowledged as one of the best horsemen in the province. Walter was given $25 or $30 and told to take the cow crew to town and show them a good time but to come back with the impounded cattle. The cowboys were delighted at the treat, and after spending the money in various Kamloops bars, they headed for home, coincidentally passing by the cattle pound. It seemed like a good time to try their roping techniques and darned if a few fence posts didn't come loose when half a dozen good cow ponies pulled on them. The cattle were driven to a far range where they wouldn't bother the good people of Kamloops again, and the cowboys retired for the night, none

Branding cattle on the Campbell Ranch near Kamloops. The man in the middle with angora chaps is Lewis Campbell Junior, and Walter Campbell is the rider on the right.

the worse for wear. In a strange twist of fate, that same night the CPR train had been held up by the famous train robber Bill Miner. When the police rode out in the morning to investigate, they found a number of horses sweated up and were sure that they had found the robbers. It took some fast talking on Walter's part to convince them that this was not the case. When they finally assured Police Chief Fernie that they were innocent, the Campbell cowboys saddled up and accompanied him on his search for the robbers.

Campbell died in 1910. Despite the fact that all his sons were fine cattlemen, the estate was eventually broken up and sold to various other ranchers. His memory lives on in the creek named after him and in his old summer range called the Campbell range.

Johnny Wilson

John Wilson, born in 1832 in Kirby-Hebben, a little English town on the border of Yorkshire and Westmoreland, was the child of gypsies, and much of his early life was spent travelling with his parents through Westmoreland, Durham and Yorkshire. He received a rudimentary schooling that stood him in good stead throughout his life and learned a little about the cattle business by helping on various farms in his home area. Although the Wilson family had been settled in the north of England for centuries, they were inherently restless. So, at the age of 17, Johnny travelled to North America, ending up in Logansport, Indiana, in 1849. There he met his future lifelong friend, Lewis Campbell, who was destined to share his fortunes and successes. The young men spent two years working on a farm in Indiana before deciding to try their hands in the gold fields of California. Wilson travelled via the Isthmus of Panama, but his dreams of instant wealth in California were shattered. After working on the American River, the Russian River and at Petaluma, where he worked for wages at a number of camps, he eventually returned to San Francisco.

His lust for gold lay dormant until he heard about the gold discoveries

Roundup in the Nicola Lake area. The horse-drawn wagons indicate that the cattle buyer and perhaps a few ranchers are on hand to look at the herd.

in British Columbia, and in 1858 he headed north with the other gold seekers from California and Oregon, all dreaming of making their fortune. Never afraid of hard work, Wilson engaged in trading on the Fraser River and then once more turned to prospecting, eventually ending up on the famous Tinker Claim on Williams Creek. After two seasons, this immensely successful claim had provided him with the capital to set himself up in a more steady line of work. Noticing that beef was selling for a dollar a pound at Williams Creek, he decided to exploit his experience in the cattle business. He once again linked up with Lewis Campbell, who by then had set himself up on a small ranch on the South Thompson River east of Fort Kamloops. The two men went into partnership and, in 1865, travelled to Oregon to purchase a herd of cattle. Campbell's ability to handle cattle, coupled with Wilson's shrewd business sense and eye for good cattle, made for an excellent combination, and the two men were very successful in the booming years of the Cariboo gold rush.

The partners originally held their cattle on Campbell's land on the Thompson, but Wilson saw the potential for ranching in the lush bunchgrass ranges of the B.C. interior and began to purchase land there. He initially took up land at Eight Mile Creek in the Cache Creek valley, a few miles north of Ashcroft. By 1897, he owned 1,000 acres there, and in 1868 he acquired 160 acres of good land at Grande Prairie (now Westwold). A few years later he increased his holdings at Grande Prairie to 1,200 acres of excellent grazing and hay land.

Wilson married a Shuswap woman named Nancy, and the two had a large family. Nancy had been involved with her people in gardening on the meadowlands near Savona's Ferry, known to this day as the Indian Gardens. Wilson purchased this land and added to it over the years until it totalled 1,400 acres. They called the property Indian Gardens Ranch, and the Wilsons occupied it for part of the year, spending the rest of the year on their land near Cache Creek.

Although John Wilson was not an overtly religious man, he was a strong believer in the faith of his forefathers and in the moral code it represented. He believed the church had a place in the community, and as Savona didn't have a church, he sought to rectify the situation. He provided a site and the cost of construction for the building of an Anglican church, asking only that it be called St. Hilda's, which was a common name in the English counties of Westmoreland, Durham and Yorkshire.

Wilson was a profligate buyer of cattle. During the 1870s and 1880s, he would ride up the Cariboo road and into the Nicola Valley with saddlebags full of gold coin and gold dust. The jingling of this coin in his saddlebags was a strong incentive to those with whom Wilson was dealing. Keeping the jingling in the background, he would ride through the herd for sale and cast a keen eye over the cattle. Joe Walters, who used to ride with Wilson told of these sales:

> Johnny'd ride through a bunch of animals with the owner, and point out the old cows and scrubby steers one after the other, and shake his head dolefully. He'd never let on he saw the fat stuff at all, but he did, all right. He'd make a fair enough offer for the lot, but never what the owner expected.
>
> When Johnny made his bid, though, he stayed with it. His word was good. There weren't many cattle buyers in his day, and he could have boosted his profits plenty, but he believed in letting the other fellow have his fair share. At that, Johnny Wilson did all right.[2]

Johnny's saddlebags full of gold were common knowledge throughout the Cariboo, and it was only a matter of time until some desperados decided to relieve him of the extra weight. He usually rode alongside a cowboy for extra protection, but on one occasion the cowboy had dropped some distance behind when a masked horseman stepped out of the woods on some lonely Cariboo road and demanded the saddlebags. Wilson didn't hesitate. Immediately he let out a wild yell and put his spurs to his horse. He wasn't scared, just smart. He realized he could get away safely before the thief could wheel his horse around. He was out of sight before the robber could sneak back to the Jack pines with the cowboy in hot pursuit.

By the 1890s, as good roads and banks became more common, Wilson exchanged his saddlebags of gold for a suitcase of money carried in a buckboard. Every summer in the 1890s he would travel by buckboard to the Chilcotin and buy all the cattle for sale. From there he would drive them to his lands near Savona to pasture them until they were marketable, which sometimes took up to five years. The Wilson drives were notorious for "absorbing" other cattle into the herd as they passed through the open ranges, and it was not unusual for the drives to finish up with more cattle than they had started out with.

In the 40 years that he sold and raised cattle in the interior, Wilson became one of the most successful ranchers in the industry and was referred to as the B.C. Cattle King. He continued ranching right up to the end, dying in the Ashcroft Hospital in 1904. His funeral was held in Savona and hundreds of his friends among the Natives and Whites of the area attended. The little church of St. Hilda was filled to overcrowding.

The Harpers: Sibling Entrepreneurs and Cattle Kings

The flamboyant Harper brothers, Jerome and Thaddeus, did everything in a big way, including the acquisition of land. From their small beginnings as drovers, they quickly became the biggest landowners in British Columbia, pre-empting and purchasing thousands of acres of prime grazing land throughout the interior. Contemporary land legislation specified that pre-emptors had to be British citizens, but the Harpers, American citizens even after the Civil War had destroyed their beloved Confederate States, proceeded to occupy and receive Crown grants of lands throughout the interior from the time of the gold rush.

Jerome Harper was the dominant brother and the driving force behind the wholesale acquisition of land and other ventures. History has judged him to be the businessman of the family, but this may be unfair to Thaddeus. Jerome occupied land east of Kamloops on the north side of the Thompson River as early as 1862, which formed the nucleus

Jerome Harper was a flamboyant entrepreneur and passionate Confederate.

of what is still known as the Harper Ranch. The brothers added to their original pre-emptions with a number of other parcels obtained through purchases and transfers. Thaddeus also acquired 544 acres of land on the south side of the Thompson River, giving the brothers a total of 3,957 acres held east of Kamloops.

As their cattle interests grew, the Harpers purchased several other large tracts of lands farther west and north and closer to the Cariboo market where the brothers had interests in a slaughterhouse near Barkerville. In 1867, Jerome bought Charles Danielson's place at Quesnelle Mouth (present-day Quesnel). The brothers used the property's 216 acres to pasture cattle bound for Barkerville. Four years later they secured the 906 acres near Cache Creek now known as the Perry Ranch and later acquired Edward Kelly's ranch in the Cut-Off Valley near Clinton. Thaddeus purchased another 14,517 acres in 1884, increasing the Kelly Ranch to a total of 14,797 acres. In January 1873, Jerome Harper took over the mortgage on Hat Creek Ranch on the Cariboo Road, just north of Cache Creek. This famous stopping house, which still stands next to Highway 97, was leased out to various operators who paid an annual rent, and the Harpers used the land for holding cattle.

However, the shrewd Harpers did not restrict their entrepreneurial interests to the cattle business. When he first arrived in British Columbia in 1859, Jerome had operated a sawmill at Yale. Showing his usual "after the fact" attitude, in 1863 Jerome applied for the right to purchase five acres of land adjoining the townsite of Yale to erect a sawmill. The local magistrate apparently refused permission because six months later a traveller to the Cariboo reported that "Harper's new saw mill at the Mouth of Quesnel had commenced work."[3] About two years later an announcement appeared in the *Cariboo Sentinel* that the Harpers, in partnership with Gustavus B. Wright, were planning to erect a flour mill at Quesnelle Mouth and were selling off their steam sawmill equipment.[4] Jerome had purchased the land of Norwegian Charles Danielson at Quesnelle Mouth, but the flour mill did not materialize and the partnership dissolved. Undeterred, in 1868 Jerome formed a new partnership with Hoiten Scott to set up a flour mill a few miles south of Clinton. Not surprisingly, it seems that Jerome did not secure title for the land on which the flour mill was situated or for water rights on the creek. Scott soon withdrew from the enterprise and Jerome was in full control. The mill remained there until Jerome's death when Thaddeus moved the mill structure and machinery to the mouth of the Bonaparte River, apparently in anticipation of the construction of the CPR along the north bank of the Thompson River. But the CPR ran along the south bank of the

Thompson and the mill was isolated. However, it continued to operate until 1890. During the entire time of operation, neither Harper brother held title to the land on which the mill was located.

Thaddeus Harper was left on his own when Jerome left British Columbia in the early 1870s. Jerome contracted a severe illness and was forced to seek expert medical attention in San Francisco. The city offered a number of temptations for a young man with unlimited finances, and Jerome indulged fully, perhaps knowing that his time was limited. His association with one of the ladies who ran one of San Francisco's best-known brothels was common knowledge. As the story goes, Jerome became quite insane towards the end, leaving one to suspect that his fatal illness may have been syphilis. In December of 1874, Jerome was found dead in a bathtub.[5] His will named Thaddeus as his executor, and his estate was valued at $150,000, although news accounts at the time of probate placed the total value of his property at more like $300,000. Thaddeus probated the will in 1875, but relatives in Virginia contested it on the grounds that Jerome was insane at the time of its execution. The case was unsuccessful, and Thaddeus took over all of Jerome's assets in British Columbia.

During the 1870s, Thaddeus became involved in a number of mining enterprises in the Cariboo. He was a partner in claims on Lowhee Creek and on Lightning Creek in the heart of the gold fields. Later he acquired a large number of leases on the Horsefly River. The *Annual Report of the Minister of Mines* for 1885 stated: "The ground all around the China Company's claim is held under lease by Mr. T. Harper, which prevents considerable prospecting being done there this winter. There has not been any work done upon the ground by Mr. Harper since the lease was obtained." Thaddeus does seem to have conducted some activity on the claims over the next few years, though, importing hydraulic equipment and employing a large crew of men to test the ground. Always a gambler, he established one of the first hydraulic mines in the Cariboo, and the mining community established around his claims became known as Harper's Camp. Despite heavy investments, however, the claims failed to return a profit and Thaddeus disposed of the leases by 1891. The town and post office retained the name Harper's Camp until 1921 when it was given its current name of Horsefly.

The brothers' greatest land purchase, and part of their enduring legacy, was Thaddeus's purchase of the lands that came to be known as the Gang Ranch. The area seems isolated now, but in the early gold-rush days, the first trail into the Cariboo was via Lillooet along the "River Trail" on the east side of the Fraser River. Drovers would winter cattle in the bunchgrass ranges north of Lillooet along the river. The area around Dog Creek had been a popular wintering place for the drovers and the Mexican packers who ran the pack trains into the Cariboo during the summer mining season. During the early 1860s the Harpers had held their cattle in this area and had taken up land on Dog Creek Mountain. The vast stretches of grasslands across the Fraser probably caught their entrepreneurial eyes, but the inaccessibility of the area made them hesitate—cattle would have to be driven across the Fraser River to the main roads and trails before travelling to market. The pragmatic brothers therefore concentrated their land acquisition elsewhere, and despite numerous accounts to the contrary, it is unlikely that they took up land west of the Fraser until at least the 1870s. By 1884, when Thaddeus Harper purchased 18,912 acres of land from the government in the Chilcotin district, the Gang Ranch was well established. Unfortunately, the last 10 years of Thaddeus's life were tragic. According to A.W. McMorran, who was the manager of the Gang Ranch in 1939, Thaddeus "was kicked in the face by a horse on his Chilcoten [sic] ranch, which was no doubt the Gang or Harper ranch."[6] Thaddeus never fully recovered from the severe head injuries and died in Victoria in 1898.

Two Races, One Family

The early settlement years of the 1870s saw hundreds of young men take up land in the lush bunchgrass ranges and fertile valleys of the B.C. interior. They established cattle ranches and settled into their new lives. Loneliness often intruded into their lives as they were usually far away from their nearest neighbour and even farther away from regular mail from home. Tom Ellis, who settled at the foot of Okanagan Lake in 1865, spoke for many young ranchers when he wrote in his diary, "Have been alone for 10 days and am so tired of this solitude, with nothing to do. I would not mind so much if I had a good book to read." This loneliness was compounded by the lack of eligible White women on the frontier where, in the more isolated areas, there were about 100 men to every White woman.

It is therefore not surprising that many, if not most, of the early ranchers and ranch hands in the interior took Native women to live with them. Far from home and the racist attitudes that prevailed in Victorian times, it was only normal for these men to seek permanent companionship among the Native people who were their closest neighbours. These young women became devoted helpmates, quick to learn the running of a household. Not only did the women prove to be excellent companions for the young men, they also brought with them an extended family that was willing and able to assist in the ranch activities. They adapted quickly to the ways of their husbands but maintained close contacts with their own people and culture. One such woman was Lucy, a member of the Similkameen tribe, who married Frank Richter. Joseph Richter, one of her five sons, remembered her contribution to the family:

> When I was little, coal oil was brought 70 miles from Hope on the backs of horses. It was used sparingly. My mother made candles in a special mould and after the cotton wick was threaded, it was filled with our own tallow. She made soap from waste fat and lye. Some of our clothing was made from buckskin traded from the Indians. Mother fashioned it into coats, shirts and pants. Take it from me, buckskin garments are warm, soft and comfortable … I suppose that today most people would think that our early days were rough. We worked hard, we had everything we needed. We were a closely knit, affectionate family, self-sufficient, yet depending on one another, each respecting the other's worth under the guidance of wise parents.[7]

The Native women and the resulting children formed the majority of the population in the pre-railway days and were generally accepted by all. The children of the Native women and non-Native men, living far from the cities at a time when only the occasional stranger would pass by, enjoyed a life of freedom and a closeness to nature that they would remember with fondness in later years. Joseph Richter reminisced about the early days: "I shall never forget those early ranch days. The valley was all ours, our lush meadows, hay fields and miles of bunch grass range, dotted with cattle, stretched as far as we could see, to be broken here and there by snake fences. Near the house our saddle stock and milk cows grazed in the rich home pasture."[8]

Eliza Jane Swalwell (daughter of George Simpson, born in Philadelphia of Scottish Presbyterian parents, and his Native Okanagan wife) looked back on a similar time in an account of her "Girlhood Days in the Okanagan": "To me it was an exquisite pleasure as a girl to ride over this green and gracious pasture land in the mornings, and to see it stretching before me for miles with the Sand Rose lying scattered on the ground as if a fairy princess had passed that way at dawn and children had strewn flowers in her path, and

Eliza Jane Swalwell could herd cattle with the best of the cowboys.

to see the sunlight on the hills. On such occasions I have sometimes seen things, or rather sensed something, so serene and beautiful that it left me weak and weeping as I sat in the saddle."[9]

Life was not all fun, though. All the children in these families pitched in to help with the ranch work and girls were not exempt:

> Before the arrival of the wagon road every one had to learn to ride, as it was the only means of getting anywhere, and we girls were all proficient horsewomen. We could round up a band of horses, drive them into a corral, rope the one we wanted and saddle him up as expertly as a man could do it … The two great events of the year were the coming of the cattle buyers in May and September. They usually sent word ahead to let us know they were coming, and then we all got busy, and everyone, girls as well as men, assisted in the round-up. On these occasions we girls felt that we were coming into our own. We could handle a horse about as well as the men, and we could show them that we amounted to something more than a mere nuisance about the place, as they sometimes seemed to think we were.[10]

A list of the ranchers who lived with Native women reads like a who's who of the early ranching community. Ranchers such as J.C. Haynes, Forbes Vernon and Cornelius O'Keefe in the Okanagan Valley, along with John Allison and Barrington Price in the nearby Similkameen, all had Native wives. The same was the case in the Cariboo, where Herman Otto Bowe, founder of the Alkali Lake ranch, and Louis Antoine Minnaberriet, founder of the Basque Ranch, were both married to Native women. While most of these men chose to live in a common-law relationship with their Native partners, there were a significant number who made their liaison official with a marriage.

The children seemed to embody what were seen as the best qualities of both races. Eliza Swalwell observed that:

> I do not know whether this responsiveness to certain beautiful aspects of nature comes to me from my Indian mother or from my father's side. It seems to me the whites are too much bound and limited, too enslaved by their written creeds and confessions of faith … Standing as I do between the two races I could never see that intellectually the Indians are not the equals of the whites. The Indians are sadly lacking in culture; that is to be seen at a glance, but social grace and refinement are things which can be acquired … Why should any man, whether Indian or white, be commiserated because he sees in the workings of nature manifestations of the Creator? He would be a dolt if he did not.[11]

Maria Brent, the daughter of Charles Houghton and his Okanagan wife, Sophia, was also keen to point out the advantages of the two heritages that she possessed. She wrote:

> They seem to possess a certain mental aloofness, a freedom and independence of judgement which makes them different from the whites, pure blood; and these qualities make for leadership among men. The half breed will either live entirely to himself, or, if he takes part in community life at all, he is apt to forge to the front. These men are in a sense "well born." They, on the one side of the house at least, have descended from a race of men who for many generations never knew what it was to receive a command from another and feel that they were under compulsion and bound to obey that command. Always they were free men, and, they will say, blood will tell.[12]

But as the interior of British Columbia opened up to more and more settlers, couples in mixed-race relationships began to find themselves in the minority and subject to discrimination. White men who had not formalized their relationship through marriage, especially those who had arrived early in the interior and were owners of extensive lands and "pillars of the community," were pressured to discard their Native concubines. This ugly discrimination that newcomers evinced against the men with a Native wife (referred to sneeringly as "klootch," for the Chinook word for "woman") is typified in the reminiscences of Sydney Russell Almond, recorded some years later but still revealing a disappointingly common attitude. He says of early Similkameen rancher Barrington Price: "He came of a good family in England and evidently had rich connections ... He married a klootch and wrote home to his friends that he had married an Indian princess. I don't know what idea his friends had of an Indian princess as they come in British Columbia, but it is safe to say that they had no such picture of her as the actual Indian klootch as we know here, even when married to a self-respecting white man."[13]

Time did not lessen the discrimination, and it seeped into the public domain as well. Henry Bigby Shuttleworth, the son of a major English landowner Lord Shuttleworth, had married a Native woman when he arrived in the Similkameen in the 1870s. Some years later he was looking for a teaching position and, after being turned down for several openings, wrote, "I suppose it is because I have an Indian Woman but I can assure you and if necessary prove to you that I am lawfully married to her."

Inevitably, as more and more White women arrived in the area, the pressure became overwhelming and led to a discreet hiding of the Native woman and her children at best or, more commonly, the man would simply reject his Native wife and remarry with a White woman. Edward Tronson owned the Vernon Hotel and experienced much discrimination by newcomers over Nancy, his wife of many years, and their six children. He features in *Valley of Youth*, written by C.W. Holiday, who came to the Okanagan in the 1880s. Holiday describes Tronson as: "a courtly-groomed old gentleman. But to see him in church looking rather like a saintly old patriarch you would never have suspected that on his ranch he maintained an Indian wife and a large half-breed family; a quite separate establishment, none of them ever appeared in public with him."[14]

Another example is William Pinchbeck, whose ranch was located at Williams Lake. In 1884, at the age of 54, he returned to his native England and married. Upon his return, he built two houses, a beautiful two-storey house, "the finest in the Upper Country," for his white wife and a smaller home, located some distance down the lake, for his Native "common law" wife and family. However, there were men who resisted the pressure from the less-accepting newcomers and who lived contentedly with their Native wives despite being ostracized by their communities. Frank Richter, probably because he was the biggest rancher in the Similkameen, stayed with his wife, Lucy, for many years. But eventually even he succumbed to the pressure, which we might now call a mid-life crisis, by marrying a 17-year-old White woman, Florence Louden, in 1894 when he was 56 years old. According to Louden's brother, Richard, however, Richter did not discard Lucy completely: "Immediately after his marriage to my sister, Richter established a home for Lucy and provided for her as long as she lived. She

Native men such as these were natural cowboys. The saddle in the foreground is a "loop seat" type with square holes cut in the seat for easier access to the stirrup leathers.

never wanted for anything … Lucy, the Indian wife, died in about 1903 or 1904 in the cabin she lived in on the original Richter Ranch."[15]

Unfortunately this was not a common outcome and many children of these families found themselves rejected by both of their races. Rejected by the White community, they often turned to their Native relatives on the reserves who treated them with suspicion and disdain. Boys at least had the advantage of being accepted on the ranches where they were readily employed as cowboys and labourers. However, many of the rejected children went on to be successful and contributed much to the ranching community of British Columbia. Some of the great cowboys of the turn of the century were the offspring of White men and Native women. Joe Coutlee, the famous cow boss of the Douglas Lake, and also George Shuttleworth, were among the many who went on to leave a legacy in the ranching community and many of their descendants are still contributing to the British Columbia ranching community today.

Susap

Susap, also known as Yankin or Sillitoe, was an Okanagan Native who was well known throughout the South Okanagan and Similkameen as a cowboy and packer. He was born around 1843, and was one of three brothers who made their mark in the region as honourable, honest men and excellent stockmen. One of his brothers, Baptiste, became chief of the Inkameep band in 1907. Susap went to work for Barrington Price in the Keremeos area in 1872 and rapidly gained a reputation as an accomplished horseman and diligent worker. Before long, John Carmichael Haynes asked him to come work for him at his ranch in the Osoyoos area. Susap took over the care and training of Haynes's large herd of horses. He was an outstanding rider and could handle and break the most difficult of horses.

Susap soon proved himself indispensable to the Haynes family. When the Haynes house caught fire in 1878, it was Susap who rushed into the burning house and carried the Haynes children, Hester and Val, to safety. A few years later, he was out on Osoyoos Lake with two of the Haynes children when he saw little Will Haynes fall into the lake and disappear under the surface. Susap dove into the lake, swam to the drowning child and pulled him out of the water. He tipped the boy upside down to let water pour out of his boots and mouth then ran with him to the house where he revived him and wrapped him in a warm blanket. The Haynes family expressed their gratitude by giving Susap a new outfit of clothes and boots every Christmas.

Susap's skills with horses made him an excellent packer, and he was regularly entrusted with taking a pack train to Hope and back over the Dewdney Trail for supplies for the Haynes family and other South Okanagan and Similkameen ranchers. In 1880, after taking cattle to Hope over the Dewdney Trail, he became the guide and packer for Bishop and Mrs. A.W. Sillitoe from Hope to Osoyoos over the trail. The trip is recorded in Mrs. Sillitoe's diary and she mentions Susap's ability to weave a bed of cedar boughs, "in the spreading of which the Indians are adepts. If skilfully laid, they form a very easy, springy bed, but woe betide the unfortunate traveller who tries to sleep on a brush bed not scientifically spread."[16] Susap, for some time afterward, was referred to as "Sillitoe" in memory of his services to the Bishop.

When J.C. Haynes died in 1888, Susap went to work for other ranches in the South Okanagan. He married Sophie and had two children, Manuel and Margaret. Susap lived to be 106 years old, and he was esteemed by both Natives and Whites as one of the best horsemen and honest workers in the area.

Antoine Allen

Antoine Allen was born in 1855 in the Willamette River Valley in Oregon Territory, the son of a White miner and his Native wife. In 1864, he travelled with Jerome and Thaddeus Harper on one of their cattle drives to British Columbia and remained with them for many years afterwards. They taught him the cattle trade, and he worked for them on their ranches west of Kamloops and in the Cariboo.

Allen was one of the drovers on the drive that Thaddeus Harper organized to relieve the range of an overabundance of cattle. The drive started in May in the Dog Creek and Alkali Lake areas and worked its way to Kamloops and through the Okanagan to the United States. The cattle were driven across the border at Osoyoos Lake and then were forced to swim the Columbia River at the mouth of the Okanagan. From there the drive proceeded south through the Grande Coulee and crossed the Snake River near Fort Walla Walla. By then the drive had been going for almost seven months, and Newman Squires, who was in charge of the drive for Thaddeus Harper, decided to winter the cattle. Only a few men remained to winter herd the cattle, and Allen returned to British Columbia with many of the other cowboys.

Antoine Allen remained in the Kamloops area. In 1881, he was working for James Todd on the South Thompson River east of Kamloops, and some years later appears to have worked for Thaddeus Harper on the Gang Ranch.

In 1910, the now-married 55-year-old Allen took part in another major cattle drive. Ulysses Campbell, son of rancher Lewis Campbell, recruited him in Kamloops to be one of the head cowboys in a drive to supply beef to the construction camps of the Grand Trunk Pacific and the Pacific Great Eastern Railways (now the B.C. Railway). Pat Burns held the contract, and after an experimental drive from the Chilcotin to Hazelton led by Joe Paine had proven successful, Burns had contracted Ulysses Campbell to take a series of drives north. Allen and the other cowboys took the train to Ashcroft to collect the saddle and pack horses that Burns had sent from Alberta. The cowboys spent a couple of weeks gathering cattle from all over the Chilcotin and assembled a herd of 800 steers at Riske Creek. The steers were carefully inspected and 300 of them culled from the herd. On May 10, the drive of 500 picked steers left the Chilcotin. It took eight days to reach Quesnel. They then battled through another 500 miles of brush and mud holes to reach Hazelton where Burns and Company had a slaughterhouse. That year, Allen accompanied another three drives of cattle, taking a total of 2,000 head to Hazelton. He remained involved in the drives until 1913, when a total of 12,000 head of Chilcotin cattle reached market.

Antoine Allen was with the Harper brothers on one of the first cattle drives into British Columbia and was still involved with driving cattle in 1913.

He retired on a wave of success and lived in the Kamloops area near his three daughters until his death in 1936. Allen was one of the true pioneer cowboys who saw the cattle industry grow and change in the interior of British Columbia.

Joe Coutlee

Joe Coutlee was the son of Alexander Coutlie (note the original spelling), a French Canadian from Trois Rivières who had settled in the Nicola Valley in 1873 and married a Native woman. At the age of 10 young Joseph's real job was working cattle for Joseph Castillion, the Mexican packer who was one of the original settlers in the Nicola Valley. He came to work at the Douglas Lake Cattle Ranch at the age of 23 in 1892 under cow boss Joe Payne and stayed there for the next 53 years. Coutlee learned the cattle trade well under the sharp eye of Joe Payne, and when Payne left in 1896, Coutlee took over as cow boss of the Douglas Lake Cattle Ranch, a position that he was to hold until his death in 1944.

Coutlee had an incredible ability to read the range. He could eye up a field and accurately predict just how many head of cattle could graze that field and for how long. This ability allowed him to carefully manage the precious bunchgrass resource that sustained the Douglas Lake cattle. He always separated the herd and moved each group to the higher elevations in the summer so that no one range was overgrazed. Coutlee knew his stock as if they were his children, even when the Douglas Lake was running 13,000 head of mixed Shorthorn and Hereford. He could remember which cows had been pulled out of mud holes two years before and where certain calves were born.

Coutlee was a large man, over 200 pounds and close to six feet tall. His cowboys referred to him as "Roaring Bill" and when he was crossed he lived up to his nickname. He expected his twenty-odd cowboys to ride any horse they were given, break, shoe and care for it, and repair its tack, not to mention rope cattle, repair fence and cook for themselves if required. Many a cowboy was sent packing who failed to live up to Coutlee's expectations. Coutlee married a Native woman, Mary Ann Horne, whom Joe affectionately nicknamed "Muggins." The two had a stormy relationship, especially when Joe was on a drinking spree when the work was all done, but Muggins stayed with him all his life and cared for their six children. She predeceased him, and when Joe died in 1945 he was buried alongside her in the Native cemetery at Shulus, close to his childhood home. His legacy to the Douglas Lake Ranch was expressed by his long-time boss, Frank Ward: "With all his failings he was a tower of strength to me especially in my early days, and I thank God he lived through my reign at Douglas Lake for he made it that much more

Hans Richter was one of the great horsemen of the British Columbia interior. He is wearing a pair of high boots with "mule ear" pulls, typical of the early cowboys.

simple … enabled me to get away from time to time and know that the cattle at any rate would be properly looked after. I never went off for a long voyage without having old Joe promise me he would not get off on a drunk during my absence, and to my knowledge he never did."[17]

John (Hans) Richter

Hans Richter was born in 1878, the fifth and youngest son of Francis Xavier "Frank" Richter, pioneer cattleman of the Similkameen Valley, and his Similkameen Native wife, Lucy. All the Richter sons were born at the "R" Ranch, which Frank sold to R.L. Cawston in 1884, moving his family to the Lower Ranch in what came to be known as Richter Pass. Hans was sent to school at the Okanagan Mission (later Kelowna) and boarded with the family of early settler Frederick Brent, returning home in the summer months to help with the ranch work. In 1892, Hans began attending the newly constructed school in the Similkameen Valley, even though it entailed a nine-mile ride in each direction. It was, perhaps, on these long daily rides that Hans developed his love of horses. As he grew older, he enjoyed working with horses, and when the first rodeos were held in the southern interior of British Columbia, he was an avid participant, winning many trophies, buckles and medals.

Rodeo was in its infancy. There were few rodeo grounds, so people would park their wagons or vehicles in a circle to form a makeshift arena. Bucking horses would be snubbed to a post, blindfolded and then saddled.

The earliest rodeos took place out on the open range where the horse or bull was roped and snubbed until a cowboy could mount. The ensuing ride could cover a great distance.

The rider would mount, the blindfold would be removed and the horse was untied. Then the fun would begin. In those days, bucking horses would be ridden until they stopped bucking, so rides often lasted for many minutes. They were not the eight-second rides of today. When the horse had been ridden to a standstill, the pick-up man would ride alongside and help the rider dismount. A good pick-up man was essential, and Hans was acclaimed as one of the best pick-up men and ropers on the rodeo circuit.

It was only natural that Hans should begin to raise his own bucking string from the wild horses he captured in the areas adjoining Richter Pass. He eventually owned a string of 40 or more bucking horses that he would supply to rodeos in Vernon, Kelowna, Penticton, Grande Forks and Christina Lake. Hans often trailed his bucking horses over the Dewdney Trail to rodeos in Chilliwack and Sumas and into Washington State. He even did the announcing at the rodeos, using a megaphone as he rode through the arena.

Hans was particularly proud that he once put on a rodeo in Victoria, Vancouver Island. He drove his horses over the trail to Hope and loaded them on boxcars bound for Vancouver. From there, they were put on barges and towed to Vancouver Island where they entertained the people of Victoria and its surrounding area.

Hans married Sarah Marsel, the daughter of Similkameen stagecoach driver Peter Marsel. Sarah was some 30 years younger than Hans who was in his fifties when they were wed. Coincidentally, a few years earlier, Sarah's mother, Julia, had married Hans's older brother, Charlie Richter, after the death of Peter Marsel. Hans and Sarah had four sons and six daughters. Hans continued to supply the rodeo circuit with bucking stock well into the 1940s, working the Princeton and Kelowna rodeos until he was 66 years old. He died at the age of 84 in 1961 and was followed by Sarah the next year.

The Chilcotin

The early gold seekers ventured into the centre of the B.C. interior via the Fraser River. As they panned the gravel bars of the Fraser farther and farther north, they came upon rich tributaries, such as the Quesnel, which brought them into the heart of the Cariboo gold fields. The country lying west of the Fraser River, known as the Chilcotin after the Native people who lived there, promised little for the gold seekers and was initially ignored. For years the miners headed east from the Fraser, leaving the land west of the river to the warlike Chilcotin people and occasional exploration parties seeking an easy route to the coast. But the packers and drovers of the gold rush days looked with interest across the Fraser at the vast grasslands stretching westward

The Chilcotin area in the late 1800s

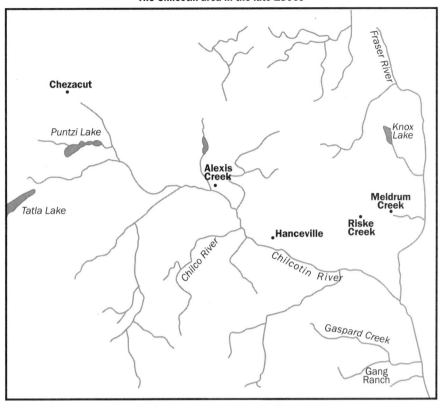

from the junction of the Fraser and Chilcotin rivers and promising some of the finest rangeland that could be found. Unfortunately, the Fraser River presented a serious barrier to the moving of cattle into the Cariboo gold fields east of the river, especially as there were no ferries.

The Chilcotin area therefore had very few ranches during the 1860s. Thomas Meldrum has the distinction of being the first White man to settle in the Chilcotin in 1866, when he followed a trail down the Fraser's west side from Soda Creek and took up land in a little valley known today as the Meldrum Valley. About the same time, L.W. Riske and brothers Sam and Ed Withrow took up land along a stream they named Riske Creek. By the end of the 1860s, Thomas Hance and Benjamin Franklin "Doc" English had established themselves 45 miles up the Chilcotin River from the Fraser where the Hanceville Post Office was established in 1889.

Everyone in the Chilcotin watched with interest the arrival of survey crews for the promised Canadian Pacific Railway in British Columbia in the early 1870s. The railway's location meant prosperity for those living along the line and, for a time, the Cariboo/Chilcotin appeared to be a likely candidate for the route. Survey crews were named by the letters of the alphabet. The various crews in British Columbia included Q and R parties that were exploring the country between the Yellowhead Pass and the Quesnel and Clearwater Lakes. Following this route would bring the new railway through the heart of the Cariboo and, with Bute Inlet on the Pacific coast being considered as a possible terminus, through the Chilcotin. In the summer of 1872, Marcus Smith, the engineer in charge of the Pacific Coast Division of the CPR, set out from Alexandria to map a route for the rail line through the Chilcotin. He explored as far as Tatla Lake, and then backtracked along the Chilanko River then along the Chilcotin River to its mouth. He set up survey camps along the way and, for a time, it looked like the railway would pass through the Cariboo and Chilcotin. Over the next few years, the surveys continued and the struggling Chilcotin economy recovered slightly by supplying beef and provisions to the crews. By the end of 1876, the survey of the Chilcotin route was completed along with a similar survey along the Fraser River. Unfortunately, the final report included the discouraging news that a railway terminus at Bute Inlet would mean eight miles of rock tunnelling. It was therefore not entirely surprising that, in December of 1877, Prime Minister Alexander Mackenzie announced that the railway would follow the Fraser River to Burrard Inlet route.

Meanwhile the Chilcotin had experienced a tremendous influx of settlers. In 1873, the provincial government declared a section of land running along the Chilcotin River open for pre-emption under the provisions of the Land Ordinance of 1870. Settlers in the early days reached the Chilcotin by ferry at Alexandria and later from Soda Creek, which was the main supply centre for the area west of the Fraser, and established themselves along the accessible parts of the lower Chilcotin River. Extensive bunchgrass ranges made the Riske Creek area particularly attractive, and land was first taken up there and then farther west to Hanceville. Later in the 1880s, the land around Alexis Creek was opened for settlement, and after the turn of the century, the area around Chezacut was settled.

Even after the completion of the railway, the Chilcotin remained inaccessible, and drovers still had to cross swollen rivers to get cattle to the railhead at Ashcroft. Hugh Bayliffe, Archie Macauley and Alex Graham, who rounded up their three- and four-year-old cattle and bought more from other ranchers, organized the first big drive from the Alexis Creek area. The 200-mile drive to Ashcroft took a month to complete. Cattle were moved slowly, at a rate of about 10 miles a day, so that they could graze on the way and not lose weight.

In early fall, the men set out with around 300 head of cattle, a few pack horses to carry supplies and spare saddle horses to replace those that went lame or drowned on the way. Food consisted mostly of bannock, beans and deer meat; their shelter was a piece of canvas, and their bed the blanket used to cover their packs during the day. They crossed the Chilcotin River to Big Creek and the Gang Ranch, and then across the Fraser River to Clinton and down the Cariboo Wagon Road to Ashcroft. Crossing creeks and rivers was slow and difficult because cattle were quite reasonably reluctant to enter the cold water. At night, two men would stay on duty for night herding as there were no corrals in which to keep the cattle. The cowboys stayed in the same set of clothing for the entire trip, drying themselves out by campfire if they got wet. When they finally reached Ashcroft, the men were a rough-looking lot, unshaven and dirty from a month on the trail, far from the popular romantic image of the cowboy. Once the cattle were loaded on boxcars, the cowboys headed for the local hotel for a bath and shave and a few drinks at the bar. In fact, they might be forgiven if they had more than just a few drinks to "wash down the trail dust." Then it was time for the long return trip to the Chilcotin before the winter snows made travel unpleasant.

Chilcotin cowboys. The young cowboys in the front are wearing standard cowboy attire, including leather "shotgun" chaps, as opposed to the older cowboy in the background, who appears to be wearing moccasins.

Most of the ranchers in the Chilcotin acquired land along the Chilcotin River and also purchased meadows on the uplands for hay cutting or summer and fall grazing. However, these meadow lands often lay on the other side of the river, and cattle had to swim across the water in both directions. At least in the spring the cowboys could rope the calves and take them across in a boat. Their bawling would bring the cows plunging into the river to come to the aid of their calves, and soon the entire herd would cross. But the late fall crossing posed more of a challenge. The cowboys would clear a trail down to the water's edge for the cattle then start them down the trail. When the cows felt the icy water, they would balk and run wildly up and down the bank. The cowboys would have to shout and holler and bang coal-oil cans loaded with rocks to force them into the water and across the river.

Finding Markets in British Columbia

The 1870s brought struggle and despair for the fledgling British Columbia ranching industry. After the exciting years of the Cariboo gold rush and the promise of growth that came with joining the new Confederation of Canada, the economy slowed to a stop. Population growth stagnated and markets for interior beef were few. The ranchers, who had entered the 1870s in a spirit of optimism, saw their herds grow and their markets shrink. Many established themselves sufficiently during the gold rush to let their herds increase as they awaited the long-promised railway, but there were others who could not hold on, especially those in the Thompson and Okanagan regions who were far from markets in the mining areas and along the Cariboo Road.

Nature also felt the effects of the downturn. The over-stocked ranges caused a significant depletion of the once-thick bunchgrasses, especially in those areas along the trails into the Cariboo. Constant grazing and trampling down of the grasses by passing herds of cattle and horses harmed the sensitive bunchgrass. Abundant grass on the other ranges meant that cattle could be moved around to give the grasslands a chance to rejuvenate but, along the roads, more sagebrush and less bunchgrass became the norm.

The ranchers recognized the effect of constant grazing on the grass and determined not to let it happen on their ranges. But what to do? They needed to find new markets and reduce the numbers of cattle. New Westminster and Victoria offered a glimmer of hope but, while they supplied some outlets for the beef, the trails were long and usually rough.

The Victoria *Colonist* saw the difficulties that the inland ranchers faced. It was a sad fact, it said, that the cost of transporting cattle from the interior made the cost of beef uncompetitive. It also believed the answer lay in the

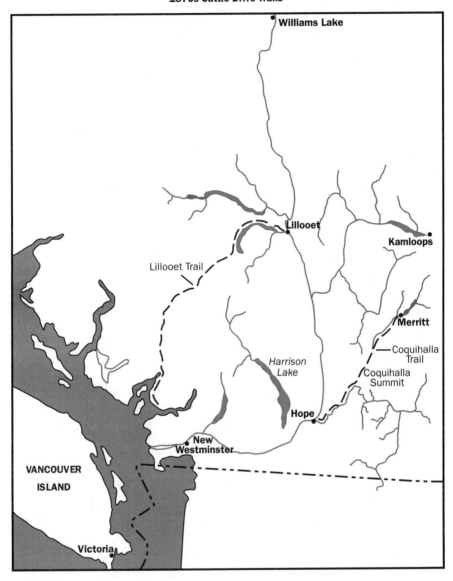

construction of a road from Lillooet via Pemberton Meadows to Squamish and then over the mountains to Burrard Inlet. "It is the only apparently available avenue through which the stockraisers east of the Cascade Range may find an outlet for the produce of their industry, on the one hand, and through which, on the other hand, the communities on the seaboard might be supplied with domestic beef. The large stock-farming interests of the interior are paralysed for want of such an outlet; and the large communities on the seaboard are, from the same cause, consuming foreign beef in payment of which the country is being drained of its wealth at the rate of something like $125,000 a year."[18]

It took four years of political wrangling and the begrudging release of provincial funds to complete a road that terminated at a point on Burrard Inlet between the Seymour and Lynn rivers by October 1877. Although the road was not completed until late in the season, when snow in the high passes was already starting to accumulate, residents of the Lillooet area were eager to try it out. Among others, Richard Hooey was convinced that the trail would make Lillooet the most important city in the interior. He had been a strong advocate of the trail and was constantly frustrated with the delays in its completion. Despite the lateness of the season, he and his partner, Robert Carson, enlisted help from a local Native man, Pecullah Kosta, and decided to drive a herd of 200 head to the coast on the new road. They set out over the rocky trail with their cattle strung out in single file and their pack horses loaded with enough food to see them to the coast. The drive to the coast was easy enough, and the trail provided sufficient feed for the cattle along the way. The trail was adequate, if rocky, although the section above Cheakamus Canyon was steep and extremely rough, and Hooey's expedition reached Squamish with their herd intact and in good health. But this had been the easy part.

The trail from Squamish to the mouth of the Seymour River on Burrard Inlet was incredibly rough, and the winter rains rendered it a sea of mud in places. The cattle suffered terribly from the constant wet, and the swollen creeks littered with numerous fallen trees made for slow going. Feed became scarce and the weary cattle lost weight rapidly. By the time they reached Burrard Inlet, the cattle were skinny and trail worn, but not one cow had been lost in the long journey. Their view across Burrard Inlet to the smoky little settlement of Gastown offered little encouragement to the drovers. The small village showed no signs of the boom city it would become within 10 years and offered no hope of a major market. A few head could be sold to the locals, but the best option was to winter the cattle and hope for a spring market. The cattle were taken across the inlet a few at a time to the McLeery farm, on the north arm of the Fraser, where Robert Carson spent the winter feeding and caring for them. Carson sold the remaining cattle in the spring and headed back to his ranch on Pavilion Mountain, wiser but not a great deal richer. Carson and his partner's experience prompted an inquiry that concluded the trail was not fit to drive cattle over. The north section became a seldom-used route for prospectors and hunters, and the section from Pemberton to Squamish was nothing more than a pack trail for supplies to the Pemberton Valley until the railway came through in 1924.

Today a modern highway connects Pemberton to Squamish via Whistler.

One of the better cattle trails of the 1870s was the Dewdney Trail from the South Okanagan to the Fraser River. From the middle of June until the middle of November most years the trail saw a steady stream of pack trains and cattle from the South Okanagan stock ranches of Tom Ellis, J.C. Haynes and William Lowe and the Similkameen ranches of Frank Richter, Manuel Barcello and John Allison. These men had all established ranches in the bunchgrass ranges of the south during the busy days of the 1860s and had large herds established by the mid-1870s.

Branding a calf in the South Okanagan. The pens were made from stout logs from the abundant timber on the surrounding hills and were effective in containing wild horses.

Driving from the Richter Ranch took two days to Princeton and 10 more over the mountains to Hope. From there they travelled by boat down the Fraser River to New Westminster and reloaded for Victoria. Until 1882, the Van Volkenburgh brothers, Abraham, Benjamin and Isaac, who ran butcher shops in Victoria, purchased most of the beef.

Henry Nicholson, an early settler in the Similkameen country, gave this account:

Stockraising being almost the sole industry, to be a cattleman was the aspiration of every youngster who could sit a horse, but to boss a drive was the coveted honour for the favoured few, it being no easy matter getting a band of steers across the mountains. Only the most careful herding ensured a successful drive. To the uninitiated the boss driver might appear a most mild though somewhat reticent sort of person, his answers somewhat monosyllabic, and that this disposition was the result of the occupation; but let anything go wrong with the drive, then would be seen what a reserve of eloquence he possessed. Dick Cawston as he was familiarly known was one of the most successful cattlemen of those days; having a happy jovial disposition and thoroughly understanding his business he was always able to get good hands and good work, and if things happened to go wrong, he was gifted with a flow of language that a brindle steer could understand.[19]

Ranchers in the Nicola Valley faced an even greater challenge when driving their cattle to market in the early 1870s. They could choose between three possible stock routes out of the valley, none of them very satisfactory. The first one offered the easiest travelling but was also the longest route. It involved heading 50 miles north to Kamloops and then westward over the old cattle trail to join the Cariboo Road at Cache Creek. The second route went west along the Nicola River to Spence's Bridge on the Thompson River. There the drovers had to pay to drive their cattle across the bridge to the road on the other side. The most direct route to the coast was through the high mountains on the west of the Nicola Valley to reach the Fraser River at Boston Bar. Unfortunately there was little feed along the way, and the rocky terrain was hard on the cattle. All of these routes followed the Cariboo Road through the Fraser Canyon as far as Yale, where the cattle could be loaded on steamers for the coastal market.

In 1873, Samuel and John Moore, former Overlanders who had settled at the north end of Nicola Lake in 1868, drove their cattle south to Princeton and then over the Dewdney Trail to Hope. This route was no improvement on the others, suffering from rocky going and a lack of good feed. But there was yet another way to the coast—a pack trail up the Coldwater River valley, over the Coquihalla summit and down the Coquihalla River to Hope. Although virtually impassable for cattle, it was by far the most direct route to the coast. In March 1873, the lieutenant governor received a petition signed by 91 settlers in the interior:

> The undersigned settlers of the Kamloops, Okanagan, Nicola and Cache Creek valleys, beg to petition Your Honour, for the construction of a road from the south end of the Nicola Forks, up the Coldwater Valley to the summit of the Coquihalla, thence down the Coquihalla to Fort Hope. The distressed condition of the stockraisers of the district, owing to their having no outlet by which they can drive to the now almost only beef market in the Province, together with the fact that the cattle ranges are becoming overstocked and destroyed we trust will induce you to make some efforts for our relief.[20]

The Chief Commissioner of Lands and Works authorized the exploration of three routes over the mountains from the Nicola Valley to Hope. Although the one over the Coquihalla Pass included "a very bad, rocky slide formed by immense fragments of granite" and remained partially under snow until at least June, it was the shortest route. However, it could never be a year-round wagon road. Nonetheless, a six-foot-wide trail was constructed over the 80-mile Coquihalla route and the drovers of the Nicola, Kamloops, North Okanagan and Cache Creek areas all used it to drive their cattle to market until the completion of the railway in 1885.

During the 1870s, resident ranchers in the Nicola Valley continued to stock the area with cattle as they increased and upgraded their herds. They used the Coquihalla Trail to bring cattle into the Nicola Valley and to drive marketable beef to the lower Fraser. George Mercer Dawson, the great Canadian explorer and map-maker for the Geological Survey of Canada, encountered one such drive bringing cattle over the trail to the Nicola Valley from Sumas Prairie on the Lower Fraser. This drive consisted of bred cows that would be used to augment the herds in the Nicola, and the cowboys ran into a unique problem—calves were being born along the trail. Dawson recorded the cowboys' interesting solution:

> Two very young calves, dropped by the way, were tied up in gunny sacks, all but their heads, & one fore leg each, which projected. Thus secured, they were hung one on either side of a Mexican Saddle. The drover said that he had killed two calves already as unable to travel, but that the cows always wanted to go back, & so he found it less trouble to carry them on thus. The horse seemed in no wise embarrassed by his strange load, but when the drove stopped strayed about feeding quite unconcerned. Not so the anxious mothers who followed the horse, lowing loudly, & looking earnestly at their calves as though they did not exactly know what to make of it.[21]

Epic Cattle Drives of the 1870s

Between 1858 and 1868, over 22,000 head of cattle arrived in British Columbia; until 1875, no cattle left the colony. The epic drive through the Rocky Mountains in the mid-1870s is recorded as the first importation of cattle for stockraising purposes into what would become the province of Alberta. This cattle drive was under the control of a man named John Shaw. Although little is known about the Shaw drive, enough details were recorded to allow us to piece together the story of this groundbreaking event.

Records for the 1870s do not list anyone in the cattle areas of British Columbia named John Shaw. And yet he must have had financial backing and knowledge of the country on both sides of the mountains. Sometime in the spring of 1875, Shaw assembled about 400 head of cattle in the North Okanagan with the intention of driving them through the mountains to the new market opening up in the Northwest Territories (modern-day Alberta and Saskatchewan), and hoping to eventually arrive at Fort Edmonton. This was at best a gamble and at worst foolhardy. Although some trails led through the mountains, the possibility of successfully driving cattle through the thick bush was unknown. And even once his cattle reached the east side of the Rocky Mountains, there was no guarantee of a ready market for them. There were only a handful of Whites in the vast area south of Fort Edmonton and the only White settlement was the mission of George McDougall at Morley. The majority of inhabitants were the less than friendly Blackfoot people in the south and the equally warlike Cree farther north. In 1873, the North West Mounted Police had arrived to establish a Canadian/British presence in the northern plains. Their efforts to tame the once wild frontier with law and order coincided with a trickle of settlers making their way to the extreme south of what is now Alberta.

Shaw proposed struggling through the virtually impassable Rocky Mountains and then driving his cattle into this unknown and unfriendly land. He chose a few men whose courage and stamina equalled his own and began to purchase cattle. Because of the overstocked ranges, he easily obtained all of the cattle he needed at rock-bottom prices. Soon his herd, comprising mostly two- and three-year-olds, was complete and assembled for trail branding.

He travelled south through the Okanagan valley and then, just before the United States border, east on the Dewdney Trail. This trail had originally been cut from Hope on the Fraser River to the mining area of Rock Creek east of Osoyoos in 1861, but thanks to the discovery of gold on Wild Horse Creek in the East Kootenays in 1863, it now extended through some incredibly wild and mountainous country. It was completed to Wild Horse Creek in 1864 at a cost of $74,000. Unfortunately, like most mining towns, Wild Horse Creek was virtually abandoned by the late 1860s so the trail had fallen into disuse and become overgrown in many places. As Shaw's drive pushed along this trail, the cowboys not only struggled to clear many sections with axes, they also had to swim the cattle across the mighty Columbia River twice. It took a good part of the summer to reach the Wild Horse Creek area at the foot of the Rocky Mountains. The mountain barrier before them seemed impassable, but local Natives informed them that there were ways through the Rockies … and then the fun really began.

The Kootenay people had used South Kootenay Pass for centuries as a way to get through the Rocky Mountains to the vast buffalo herds on the prairies. On their return trip, however, they had always preferred the North Kootenay Pass because its gentler slopes made it easier going for horses laden with buffalo meat. There was a third pass, the Crowsnest, but when Captain Thomas Blakison of the Paliser Expedition visited the Kootenay people in

1858, he was told that it was "a very bad road and seldom used." It is likely that the Shaw party chose the North Kootenay Pass to drive their herd of cattle through to the prairies into the heart of the warlike Blackfoot people's territory. The poor cowboys, scratched and worn from their time in the bush, rejoiced at open spaces, little realizing what trouble lay ahead.

Charles Ashton was one of the cowboys on that drive. His daughter, Minnie Ashton, later reported, "Although my father was not given to reminiscences, I have heard him tell how, on that trip on the prairies as they rode herd, they were one night nearly eaten alive with mosquitoes and on the next they had struck a blizzard that almost froze them in their saddles." Shaw and his cowboys followed the foothills and, in the middle of August, came upon the mission that the Methodist missionaries George McDougall and his son, John, had established in 1873 at what is now the townsite of Morley, west of Calgary. In later years, John McDougall recounted the arrival of the party: "During the autumn and just prior to my last trip, the first large bunch of cattle for stock-raising purposes came into the country. These were brought over the mountains from the Columbia Lakes by one John Shaw. The band consisted of some 700 head and his intention was to drive them on right to Edmonton. However on my advice he left his cattle on the Bow and rode on first to see the Edmonton country for himself. Having done this he gratefully came back and wintered beside us at Morley."[22]

McDougall's estimate of 700 head of cattle was high, but there had been an increase in numbers due to calves being born on the journey. According to a letter written at the time by John Bunn, HBC trader at Morley, the herd included 200 cows, 187 steers, 60 spring calves born along the way and 9 horses. Shaw failed to convince John Bunn to buy his herd at his asking price of $38 a head and resigned himself to spending the winter there.[23] Set in the traditional winter camping grounds of the Stoney people, Morley was ideally situated to take advantage of the warm Chinook winds that blew during the winter months.

George McDougall died in a blizzard somewhere north of Morley that winter, and his son, John, was left in charge of the mission. John Shaw saw an opportunity to use McDougall as a contact in the area which, Shaw correctly surmised, would become a major cattle raising territory. He made McDougall a proposal:

> Mr. Shaw made me a surprising offer. When we were riding down the valley together he said, "Now, John, that your father is gone you surely will not remain in missionary work any longer. I want you to join with me. I see

opportunity in this country for us, you to work on this side of the mountains and I on the other in the stock business. We can handle cattle and horses as I see it to a great profit and I will gladly give you half of all I own at once and thus we may start as equal partners.[24]

After some consideration, McDougall decided to turn down the generous offer and to continue his work as a missionary. He devoted the rest of his life to work among the Stoney people until 1907.

The cattle wintered well and managed to keep themselves well on the prairie grasses of the foothills. In the spring of 1876, Shaw rode to the newly established North West Mounted Police fort at the junction of the Bow and Elbow rivers. This outpost, initially named Fort Brisebois by its founder, Inspector E.A. Brisebois, was now known by its permanent name of Fort Calgary. Shaw managed to obtain a subcontract to supply beef to the Mounted Police at Fort Calgary during the summer of 1876. The cattle were pastured in the tall prairie grasses and gradually sold to the North West Mounted Police at a large profit.

When he had sold the last of the cattle, John Shaw decided to head out to his original destination, Fort Edmonton. He bid farewell to his cowboys and headed north. The men turned and headed back to British Columbia the same way that they had come.

When Charles Ashton arrived back in Priest's Valley, as Vernon was then called, he met and soon married Philomene Jangrau who had just arrived from Fort Colville. With the money he had made from the drive to the prairies, Ashton purchased a ranch on Swan Lake. He eventually moved up the valley to the Shuswap River where he remained for the rest of his life. The community of Ashton Creek is named after him.

Another cowboy on that drive was Francis "Frank" O'Keefe, younger brother of Cornelius O'Keefe who had settled at the head of Okanagan Lake in 1867. Frank had come out west in the early 1870s and taken to the cowboy way of life like a duck to water. He became an excellent rider, teamster and all-round cowhand. He worked for J.B. Greaves in 1881, and when Greaves set up the Douglas Lake Ranch a few years later, Frank moved with him and spent many years breaking horses for the Douglas Lake Ranch.

Other cattle drives successfully passed through the Rocky Mountains to the Northwest Territories (present-day Alberta) during the next few years before the railway connected the east and west sides of the mountains permanently. In 1884, James McConnell, manager of the Haynes Ranch in the South Okanagan, assembled a large herd of cattle in the Grande Prairie (now Grand Forks) area along the border with the United States. He and a group of mostly Native cowboys from the Inkameep Reserve drove the cattle through the Crowsnest Pass, by then open to travel, and sold them at Fort McLeod for $80 a head. This was an excellent price for cattle and probably indicated the superior breed of cattle that were found in British Columbia at the time. The original cattle in the gold rush days that had prospered on the bunchgrass of the interior had produced descendants that were a much heavier and more marketable breed of cattle than the mostly longhorn cattle being driven into the Northwest from Montana and points south. So the budding ranching industry in the Northwest continued to look to British Columbia for cattle.

The best-known and, without a doubt, longest drive out of the province was organized by Thaddeus Harper in the spring of 1876. The *British Colonist* newspaper in Victoria reported the venture:

> Beef Exportation: Mr. T. Harper proposes to take some 800 head of beef cattle from British Columbia to Chicago. He intends to drive via Salt Lake and then take the railroad. At present there are large numbers of cattle in the interior; the market is limited and a band of beef cattle would hardly realize $15 per head. At present, at Chicago, cattle will net over the cost of driving and railroad expense about $40 a head. A few shipments to that point would tend to relieve the market in the interior and consequently give stockowners a better opportunity of disposing of their cattle.[25]

Harper purchased about 800 head of cattle, from three to eight years old, in the Dog Creek, Canoe Creek and Alkali Lake areas, and by May 16 they were reported to have reached a point "a little above Clinton, bound for Salt Lake City."[26] The report also mentioned that, although a few of the animals looked poor, the majority were good beeves. The cattle were moved slowly, averaging about 12 miles a day and grazing on the spring grass along the route that ran along the old drover trail of the 1860s, across the Thompson River at Savona's ferry, along the south side of Kamloops Lake and over the height of land from Monte Creek to the North Okanagan. At the O'Keefe Ranch the cattle rested a few days, and an additional 428 head were purchased from the ranchers in the area. The drive continued through the Okanagan Valley and crossed the border into Washington State at Osoyoos. From there it followed the Okanogan River and crossed the Columbia, travelling along the trail through the Grand Coulee to eventually cross the Snake River near Walla Walla. By then winter was approaching, and Harper decided to winter his cattle and wait to see market conditions in the spring.

Other cowboys on that drive included Newman Squires, Antoine Allen, Charlie Connor, Tom Moore, Joe Tenice, Louis Eneas, Jimmy Joseph, Jimmy

Rendell (a boy) and possibly Johnny Twan and Bill Hart. Most of them carried guns on this drive, mainly because of the threat from predatory animals and perhaps to pick off a few grouse to supplement rations on the way. Among the cowboys, Newman Squires was in charge and Allen, Tenice, Eneas and Joseph were of Native or mixed-blood. Many of these men spent their lives as cowboys in British Columbia, and their names recur frequently in the stories of ranching in the province. Some of them, including Jimmy Joseph who was the last survivor, came only as far as the winter camp because only a few cowboys were needed to herd the cattle through the winter.

When spring broke and the drive was set to continue, Thaddeus Harper assessed the situation. From the Columbia River to the nearest rail transportation at Kelton, Utah, north of Salt Lake, was a drive of about 600 miles. Shipping from there to Chicago would have cost about $250 for a car of 20 head, and prices in Chicago had plummeted to between $16 and $17 for three-year-old steers, about the same as the stock had cost in British Columbia. Undaunted, Harper and his cowboys pushed on, spending the summer of 1877 in Idaho. Here the cattle were held and fattened up until Harper could decide what to do with them. Sure enough, typical of the Harpers' combination of business acumen and sheer luck, the story ended happily. The *British Colonist* reported the following February: "British Columbia Feeding California with Cattle. – Some eighteen months ago Mr. Thaddeus Harper drove from British Columbia into Northern Idaho 1200 head of beef cattle. These cattle were summered during 1877 in Idaho, where there was scarcity of neither water nor feed. The drought in California during the same year caused the death of many thousand head of stock, and now Mr. Harper's band is coming into market at San Francisco. The cattle are large and well-grown beeves, rolling in fat, and have been sold at $70 per head."[27]

Harper profited enormously from this venture and, inspired by his success, made arrangements for shipping additional cattle to San Francisco. The *Colonist* reported in April 1878: "British Columbia Oxen. An advertisement in the S[an] F[rancisco] Bulletin offers a lot of extra large tame oxen from British Columbia for sale in quantities to suit. 'Can anything good come out of Nazareth?' 'Mr. Thaddeus Harper of British Columbia has imported into San Francisco some extra large steers, selected expressly, and intended for heavy work, etc. They are larger and finer than anything usually found in California, and Mr. Harper believes they will supply a want which has heretofore been difficult to fill.'"

Thaddeus Harper is frequently judged to be less of a businessman than his brother Jerome had been, but this venture and its outcome present a significant challenge to this belief and show him as an entrepreneur of the very best.

The Range Horse

An old-time cowhand once said, "Cowboys is noisy fellers with bow legs and brass stomachs that rides hosses and hates any kind of work they can't do on one." The cowboy and the horse have been inseparable since the beginning of the cattle trade in North America. British Columbia, where the open ranges stretched unfenced from the United States border to the Cariboo Chilcotin in the early days, was no different. Cattle roamed free and spent much of their time in a half-wild state. The only way to handle these wild range cattle was on horseback, for a man on foot was at the mercy of their sharp horns and pounding feet.

The working cow horses of the early years were small, seldom over 14 hands high and no more than 600 pounds in weight, but powerful. They could run

Cowboy proudly mounted on his cow horse. The cayuses of British Columbia were among the finest for working cattle.

all day and then kick off the hat of their rider at night. They were descended from the Barb horse of North Africa that the Moors had brought to fight in Spain in 711. Unlike the bulky powerful horses of northern Europe, these horses, bred in the hot dry countryside of North Africa and Andalusia, were lean, sinewy and active. The Spanish then brought horses to North America in the 1500s and here they found an environment similar to that of their native North Africa. The hot dry climate of Mexico and the southern United States and the short grasses of the hot plains made the small lean horses even more wiry. The hundreds of horses that escaped into the wild thrived in the plains and mountains of the south and, in their wild state, grew as fleet as deer and strong as oxen. Generation after generation of horses lost flesh and gained "wind." What they lost in beauty they made up for in utility. They were made for running and quick turns with their lungs built from generations of clean air, hearts of centuries of freedom and stomachs of years of dry feed.

These superbly conditioned horses moved northward from Texas onto the plains and from California into the mountains and wet climate of the northwest. In Oregon and the Great Basin area the horses changed subtly, becoming stockier and heavier, perhaps due to the influence of the French-Norman horses brought to the area by the French-Canadian fur traders. On the ranges of the northwest, the wild horses generally became known as a "cayuses," a term unknown in the south or east of the Rockies. It derived from the Cayuse people in eastern Washington and Oregon who were noted for their expert horsemanship and careful breeding of these small, strong horses. The term came north with the early drovers and miners and came to refer to any wild horse that could be broken for ranch work. Over time, the use spread east of the Rocky Mountains, but in the early days it appears to have been unique to the northwest.

Records of duties paid on imported livestock at the Osoyoos Customs House in 1861 and 1862 show that, during these two years alone, some 3,396 horses were brought in, almost equal to the 4,817 head of cattle brought in during the same period.

One of the herds of horses driven into British Columbia at that time was purchased by George Masiker from a Mr. P. Rudio. Masiker recorded details of the drive, which started on April 27, 1862, in his trail diary which has been preserved. The herd consisted of 61 head of horses and was ferried across the Columbia River at The Dalles. The fare for the ferry was paid with one horse, valued at $47.50. From The Dalles, the herd was ferried across the Columbia at White Bluffs and again at the mouth of the Okanagon River. Instead of following the usual route through the Okanagan Valley, however, Masiker drove his herd along the Similkameen River and then north through the Nicola Valley to Fort Kamloops. The horses were held in the Lillooet area and during the next three months sold for an average of $50 a head. An interesting point is that a majority of these horses were sold to Natives in the Lillooet area. The usefulness of the horses for packing combined with the excellent wages that Native packers were earning probably accounted for the sales. Masiker returned home via the Harrison Lillooet trail to New Westminster and then to Victoria and back to Oregon.

In the interior of British Columbia, cayuses found another environment that particularly suited their constitution. Extensive grasslands and hot dry summers resembled the southern climates from whence they had come, and the cold winters were still mild enough that horses could survive by pawing away the snow in the sheltered valleys. Soon cayuses were at home in British Columbia and joined those that had escaped from the Native people and the fur traders in earlier years to form large herds of wild horses. The ranchers and cowboys of the interior saw these herds as the ready material that they needed to carry on their business. The thrill of the wild horse chase and the toughness and skill of the horse breaker became a part of the cowboy way of life in British Columbia.

Hugh B. Walkem, son of the premier of British Columbia, wrote an article for the *Ottawa Citizen* in 1881, later copied in the *Inland Sentinel* (then published in Yale), in which he described the horses and the methods of breaking used in the Nicola Valley. While noting that some of the ranchers in the Nicola Valley, including Guichon, Gilmore, Hamilton, Moore and Mickle, had brought in horses to upgrade the quality of the working horses, he comments that:

The general purpose horse of this region, however, is a "cayoosh," a small, but hardy native animal. Now the term "cayoosh" is a term of reproach, for instance if you want to make a particularly disagreeable remark concerning your neighbour's horse, just call it a "mean cayoosh," a term which implies all the vices and defects that horse-flesh is heir to. But after all the much-despised "cayoosh" is a very useful animal, and it is the mode of breaking and abusing him that makes him mean and vicious, as he generally has much less pains taken with his education than his more dignified brother, the imported American horse. The "cayoosh" is superior to the latter as a stock horse, for he is more active and not being so valuable you do not lose very much if you in any way injure him, and it does not take very long to "stiffen him up" to use a trite expression, for driving stock necessitates a great deal of hard riding. I stated that the manner of breaking the "cayoosh" had a great deal to do in causing him to be mean and vicious, and I shall give you a short description of the method usually but not universally adopted here.

A band of what one might truly call wild horses is driven into an enclosure, called a coral [sic]. A lassoer (one expert in throwing the lasso) enters the coral [sic], and awaiting his opportunity, throws a noose of a lasso around the neck of the animal he intends to break. The horse, considerably astonished as well as terrified by his novel necklace, dashes around the coral [sic] in an impetuous manner until he is snubbed by the end of the lasso being twisted around a post and the slack drawn in. As soon as the horse will allow himself to be stroked and handled he is saddled and bridled, his trainer or "breaker" as he is called, having blindfolded the "cayoosh" he proceeds to mount him. As soon as he is fairly seated in the saddle he removes the bandage from the horse's eyes, and spectators eagerly await further developments. If the animal commences "bucking" then the enthusiasm of the spectators rises in proportion to the height of the jumps or the number of evolutions gone through by the "cayoosh."

In "bucking" the animal arches his back, puts his head between his front legs, stiffens his limbs, springs into the air and comes down on "all fours" and, as I remarked in my former letter, the rider consequently receives a jar which very often sets all the conflicting emotions and feelings

of the mind considerably on the jar. The first "buck" very often suffices for some riders who, considering that the firmer but less solid position is on the ground, hurriedly dismount, not in the usual manner, however, but over the horse's head, an undignified, but speedy manner of dismounting. If he is fortunate to escape a broken neck, he may probably obtain a view of the starry heavens, no matter what hour of the day it may be. Now, a horse that is *en fait* at springing into the air and coming down as described above will vary the monotony by wheeling while in the air, so that when he reaches the ground his head will be where his tail was before, and his tail where his head had been. A spring sideways is very effective.

But to resume the subject of "breaking," after a horse has been ridden about a week's time by his trainer, he is "broken for the saddle" and is often warranted not to "buck" in the future, but such guarantee is by no means reliable.

A man who follows the occupation of "breaking horses for the saddle" is in common parlance term'd a "Buckero" or "Buckeero," (I am doubtful of the orthography).[28]

Some of the terminology in this article was unique to British Columbia. "Cayuse," for example, was used only in B.C. in the early days. Elsewhere, the wild horse was referred to as a "bronco" (from the Spanish meaning "wild") or a "mustang." Another local term was "corral," a Spanish loan word that had travelled north from California. "Corral" denoted an area enclosed by logs or pickets for breaking horses or slaughtering cattle. "Buckaroo," which derives from the Spanish *vaquero*, was used exclusively west of the Rockies and spread northward from California. All of these

Preparing to rope a horse for breaking. All is calm until the rope is thrown over the chosen horse's head, and then the excitement begins.

Preparing to break a horse. The cowboy closest to the horse is wearing "bat wing" chaps.

terms, as well as the technique of "snubbing" a horse (roping it and tying it to a post) before breaking it, were introduced from the south and illustrate the enduring influence of the Spanish *vaquero*.

As the herds of wild horses grew in the B.C. interior, events were unfolding elsewhere that would make these hardy range horses much in demand. During the early 1880s, as railway construction advanced across the prairies, cattle ranching was starting up in a big way in the southern grasslands of the Northwest Territories, the future Alberta and Saskatchewan. Demand for horses in these areas was great, and the ranches of Montana could not supply anywhere near enough horses. At the same time, the ranchers of southern British Columbia knew that there was an abundance of horses in the hills and upland areas of the province and acted quickly to profit from their knowledge. Between 1883 and 1885, thousands of horses were driven east from the grasslands of British Columbia.

In 1883, brothers John and William Roper Hull, who had settled at Edith and Hull Lakes in the 1870s, rounded up a herd of 1,200 horses in the hills south of Kamloops and drove them through the Okanagan Valley. The herd was then crossed into the United States at Osoyoos and given a temporary permit to cross U.S. territory on the way east. Normally a special envoy accompanied the herd through the U.S. at a cost to the drovers of $4 a day plus expenses to ensure that the horses were not sold in the U.S. without customs duty being charged. The Hulls and their cowboys drove the herd down the Okanogan River to Omak Lake and then across the Colville Indian Reservation. The herd was swum across the Columbia River and then via Spokane Falls to cross back into Canada at Bonners Ferry. From there they travelled through the Crowsnest Pass into the prairies. They sold many of the horses to the North West Cattle Company that ran the Bar U Ranch southwest of Calgary.

Thaddeus Harper, ever alert to the potential to make a dollar, observed the success of this drive. The following April, Newman Squires, who had been connected with the Harper family since the earliest years of their ranching

The moment of truth—the buckaroo has one foot in the stirrup and is preparing to mount the cayuse. Wild horses were blindfolded to calm them until the saddle and bridle could be secured.

enterprises, assembled a herd of 200 horses in the Dog Creek area and, accompanied by several Gang Ranch cowboys including Hector McLean, brother of the infamous McLean boys who had terrorized the interior of British Columbia in 1879, began the long drive to the Northwest Territories. On reaching Kamloops, Squires rested his horses for a couple of weeks and had a number of them shod to withstand the hard travelling ahead of them. By early May he and his cowboys were heading through the Okanagan Valley and following the same route that the Hull brothers had taken through the Crowsnest Pass. Reaching Fort McLeod, Squires and his men sold all the horses at a good price and then turned to travel back to British Columbia. The Kamloops *Inland Sentinel* reported that Newman Squires passed through Kamloops in late November on his way back to the Gang Ranch. The account also mentioned that Squires had encountered numerous people travelling over the same route, indicating that it was the main thoroughfare through the mountains at the time.[29]

Other ranchers quickly recognized the potential market for British Columbia horses in the Northwest Territories. Frank Barnard of the BX Ranch followed the same route as Squires with 350 head of horses and Arthur Best sold his ranch at Okanagan Mission to A.B. Knox and drove his horses and cattle to the ranching country east of the Rockies.

The demand for British Columbia horses for the prairies continued even after the CPR was completed. In fact, the rapid settlement of the ranching areas of the northwest and the ease of shipping stockcar-loads of horses by rail intensified the transfer of horses across the Rockies. In August of 1886, Senator Cochrane, who had established the immense Cochrane Ranch west of Calgary, met with Thaddeus Harper in Ashcroft and negotiated the purchase of 500 horses. The stamina of these stocky range horses obviously impressed Cochrane who intended to break them

Breaking wild horses in the Kamloops area. The activity is being viewed by a large number of onlookers, indicating the "entertainment value" of horse breaking.

and sell them to the British army for cavalry purposes. The horses were driven to Ashcroft and loaded on stockcars where they could be shipped to Calgary for $130 a car.

During this time, other ranchers began to import more notable breeds of horses in an effort to combine the stamina of the cayuse with the size of the larger breeds. John Gilmore of the Nicola Valley brought in two half-Norman dapple grey mares, three and four years old, to use for breeding stock to upgrade the working horses of the Nicola.

Chinook

Early British Columbia cowboys were allegedly masters of three languages, English, Chinook and profane.[30] It was no exaggeration to say that west of the Rocky Mountains, throughout the Pacific Northwest, the common language spoken by the Native people and the early settlers was Chinook, a language that consisted of a mixture of Native dialects, French and English.

Long before European contact, the Native people of the northwest spoke dozens of distinct and unique languages. In the area of present-day British Columbia, there were at least 30 languages, not including different dialects within the languages. Native people had traded for countless centuries before the explorers and fur traders arrived and it was not unusual to find sea shells and oolican grease far inland from the coastal areas where they were obtained. Trading is always easier when buyer and seller share a common language, and so a language of trade, comprising the simplest terms of expression, evolved. The earliest fur traders adapted and added to that common language so that the French *joual* of the Quebecers and Metis fur traders and the English of the Yorkshiremen and Orkney Islanders found their way into the mix. When the earliest missionaries, settlers and drovers arrived, they encountered a complete language that could be spoken to Natives or Whites anywhere in British Columbia. Even though its grammar and vocabulary were limited, the new language displayed a flexibility and power of expression that met every need of normal conversation.

Most of the early cowboys were of Native or mixed-blood origin so it was only natural that Chinook should become the most commonly spoken language of the ranches in the interior. It remained the main form of communication between Natives and Whites until well after the turn of the century. As Dorothy Hewlett Gellatly observed: "In those early days we in British Columbia, were more or less a bi-lingual race. The Custom's Officer on the wharf at New Westminster, pointing to some baggage, would say to some newly-arrived immigrant just off the boat from San Francisco, 'Are these your "iktas"?' (things), and the schoolboys at play would shout, 'Klosh nanich,' instead of 'Look out.' The children did not go to school to learn Chinook, they grew up with it."[31]

Joseph Richter, the son of Frank Richter and his Similkameen wife, Lucy, spoke the language fluently.

At first our only neighbours were Similkameen Indians. We often hired them to help in the fields or on the range. Fluency in Chinook jargon was necessary and I learned to understand but not to speak the Okanagan tongue. On one occasion, when I was trading deer hides for buckskin gloves I heard the klootchman say to her husband in Okanagan, "These are very good skins." But when he turned to me he said in Chinook, "Yaka skin tenas kloshe" (skins not much good). "Oh" [I] said, "Your klootchman just told you they were good skins." After that I got the trade I expected.[32]

Some common words for the cowboy speaker of Chinook included:

kiuatan: horse	*moosmoos*: cattle, buffalo
klootchman moosmoos: cow	*kamooks*: dog
lemel: mule	*callipeen*: rifle/musket
lope: rope	*lewhet*: whip
seapo: hat	*siskiyou*: a bobtailed horse
kishkish: to drive	*tupso*: grass
lamonti: mountain	*stick shoes*: boots

Chapter Three

THE RISE OF THE COWBOY

The Iron Horse

On May 14, 1880, almost nine years after British Columbia had entered confederation, a blast of dynamite at Yale on the Lower Fraser River heralded the beginning of construction of the CPR. Only 128 miles of the proposed railway were contracted out to Andrew Onderdonk but the implications for the ranchers of the interior were significant. Not only would the completed line provide easy access to west coast and eastern Canadian markets but the huge construction crews working on the railway would also need to eat.

The ranchers who had hung on grimly through the difficult years of the 1870s had good reason to be optimistic. Onderdonk expected to employ 5,000 men during the summer of 1881. In June, the CPR invited tenders for a large and steady supply of fresh beef for the work crews. Their requirements were so great that only the largest ranches could hope to answer their needs. Not surprisingly, Thaddeus Harper won the contract. He sold off all his surplus cattle that had accumulated since his great cattle drive of 1876 and set about purchasing all the cattle he could from Cariboo and Chilcotin ranchers. Prices for cattle began to move upward to over $20 a head, and the market for 1882 looked even more promising as railway construction reached its peak.

As the 1882 construction season approached, Joseph Blackbourne Greaves, who had settled near Savona in the 1860s, saw the potential for controlling the market. In December of 1881, Greaves had contacted Benjamin Van Volkenburgh, who operated the British Columbia Meat Market in Victoria and who had purchased cattle from Thaddeus Harper

Group of Douglas Lake Ranch cowboys, probably not one of them over 20 years old. George McLean, standing on the right, went on to win the Distinguished Conduct Medal for his bravery in the Battle of Vimy Ridge.

since 1880. Greaves convinced Van Volkenburgh that for $80,000 he could purchase enough cattle to control the cattle market in British Columbia and to guarantee obtaining the contract to supply beef to the CPR work crews for the next several years. Van Volkenburgh enlisted the support of Joseph Pemberton, William Curtis Ward of the Bank of British Columbia, Charles W.R. Thomson of the Victoria Gas Company and Judge Peter O'Reilly.

The new syndicate thus formed agreed to begin quietly purchasing all available cattle through the Thompson and Okanagan districts during the winter of 1881–82. J.B. Greaves, who was responsible for buying cattle, obtained about 2,200 head in the Nicola Valley early in the new year and sent Overlander Brock McQueen to the Okanagan Mission to buy 400 head of cattle at between $17 and $20 a head. The cattle were purchased and held on the seller's ranches until they would be needed. Greaves wrote to his partners of his intention to "get 30 or 35 Hundred Head of Cattle that will give our Compy [sic] control of the market for this season." At the same time, Thaddeus Harper, characteristically optimistic that he would win the 1882 contract for CPR beef, was purchasing cattle in the Kamloops area and intending to buy in the Okanagan and Similkameen. It was not long

Cattle of the 1880s were of mixed breeds, but an occasional white-faced Hereford can be seen in the herd, indicating the first attempts at raising purebred cattle.

before cattlemen realized that something was afoot. By April, the *British Columbian* newspaper had heard of the competition and wrote: "Corner in Beef: It is reported that some shrewd speculators have secured a corner in Mainland beef, and that in consequence meat will have an upward tendency. It is estimated that a cool $150,000 will be made out of the unfortunate consumers, unless the 'corner is broke' by some means not at present discovered."[1] The price of marketable cattle climbed steadily, eventually reaching $25 a head, and soon all three-year-old and older cattle that had been accumulating on the ranges had been sold.

Despite of the efforts of J.B. Greaves and his partners, Thaddeus Harper received the contract to supply beef to the CPR for 1882. Undeterred, the syndicate continued to buy up cattle, still hoping to control the market. Harper successfully supplied beef during 1882 and obtained a renewed contract for 1883, but his supply of cattle could not meet the demands of the CPR work crews, and in the middle of the 1883 season, the syndicate finally took over the contract. Greaves chose Angus McInnes as foreman in charge of delivering cattle to the construction crews. Once a week, McInnes and his cowboys would pick up 300 head of cattle from where they were being held and drive them to the construction area. Depending on the location of the ranches on which the cattle were being held and the location of the

construction crew, the drives would be via the Coquihalla Pass or even the Fraser Canyon.

From the middle of the 1883 season until the end of railway construction, the syndicate controlled the market and prospered just as they had hoped. Greaves continued to travel through the interior and purchase cattle well into the 1890s. Ranchers in the Okanagan, Thompson and Nicola valleys and those in the Cariboo came to trust that Greaves would pay fair prices and that his notes of credit were as good as cash. In the early years, Greaves would simply confirm a deal with a handshake and leave the cattle to be picked up later. But, as trade increased, it became obvious to the syndicate that it would be more efficient to hold the cattle in a central location for delivery. They therefore began to look for land, somewhere close to the CPR line, on which to hold their vast herds of cattle. By this time, the syndicate, through J.B. Greaves, had entered into a partnership with Charles M. Beak, who was purchasing land in the bunchgrass range of the Douglas Lake area. The Douglas Lake Cattle Company, soon to be the largest ranch in the British Commonwealth (a title it still holds today), was established in 1886 with Greaves, Beak, Thomson and Ward as partners.

The rising cattle market of the early 1880s brought financial prosperity to ranchers. Construction of the railway also promised a wave of settlement and increased demand for suitable land. So, using their new-found wealth, the ranchers expanded their land holdings as fast as they could, buying out smaller ranches and any available government land. Many ranchers took advantage of the fact that government-controlled Crown land could be purchased for one dollar per acre. Ranchers in the B.C. interior, whose holdings during the bleak years of the 1870s had averaged 1,000 acres, began to buy up all available rangeland. The provincial government, uncomfortably aware that much of the good, arable land in the bunchgrass ranges was being purchased, passed the Land Act of 1884, which raised the price of agricultural land from one dollar to $2.50 per acre and removed the provision for pastoral leases, leaving only "mountainous tracts of land, which are unfit for cultivation and valueless for lumbering purposes" at one dollar per acre. Applications already being processed under the previous land act continued to be approved under the previous regulations. Since there had been a scramble for land prior to the passing of the 1884 act, some 109,959 acres were acquired under this clause, notably by ranchers Thaddeus Harper (12,146 acres), Forbes George Vernon (4,739 acres) and Thomas Greenhow (3,460 acres).

The increasing size of ranches and quantity of cattle inevitably affected the nature of ranching, and the image of those who worked the cattle. It was no longer possible for a rancher to work his own cattle with only the help of a few riders during roundup: the amount of hay needed to winter large herds of cattle required the help of a large work crew, full-time cowboys were needed to watch and care for the cattle during the summer months when they were pastured in the uplands, and large roundup and branding crews were hired seasonally to deal with the bigger herds. The mystique of the "cowboy" captured the imagination of young men from all over the world as dime-store novels from south of the border painted a picture of a larger-than-life individual who, most usually with six-guns blazing, tamed the west. Almost incidental to this was the occasional mention of the day-to-day drudgery of tending cattle. Nonetheless, the romantic image of the cowboy as a rugged individual living close to the land prevailed.

Cattle Drives During the Railway Boom

The construction of the CPR through British Columbia encouraged the launch of a number of other major construction projects in the province.

In 1883, the Triangle Ranch in the Nicola Valley won the contract to supply 300 head of cattle every month to the Royal Navy at Esquimalt on Vancouver Island where 700 men were stationed. Donald McInnes, a 19-year-old man living in eastern Canada, received word from his brother Angus, working in the Nicola Valley, that the Triangle was looking for a foreman. McInnes jumped at the chance and travelled to British Columbia, taking the train as far as the railhead in the middle of the prairies and then riding horseback the rest of the way. He arrived in the Nicola Valley in June, and was promptly hired as the foreman of the Triangle Ranch. His formidable task was to come up with a steady supply of cattle at a time when Thaddeus Harper and J.B. Greaves were also scouring the country for cattle to secure the lucrative CPR contract. McInnes travelled throughout the interior looking for marketable cattle and recruited a group of excellent Native cowboys to help him round up the cattle and drive them to a holding area at the Triangle Ranch. As he later recalled, he "rode all the main trails from Spence's Bridge to Kelowna, and from Similkameen to the Chilcotin." Many a time the cowboys would have to pitch their tents wherever night overtook them. Night herders were stationed to hold the cattle then everyone moved on the next morning to another ranch.

Once the cattle had all been assembled at the Triangle, McInnes would make two drives a month with 150 cattle on each trip. Accompanied by five Native cowboys, he would drive the cattle over the Coquihalla Trail to Hope. It was not unusual to lose a few head on the narrow trail, barely wide enough for cattle to travel in single file, and with one side a wall of rock and the other a drop of 300 feet. There was also a dangerous river crossing on the

Coquihalla Trail where a narrow bridge of three logs laid side by side formed a makeshift bridge. Cattle frequently fell off the bridge, and on one trip alone, McInnes lost 11 steers on the narrow trail and even narrower bridge. Once the drive reached Hope and the cattle were loaded on a river steamer, the Native cowboys would head back to the Triangle and McInnes would continue to travel with the cattle to New Westminster and Victoria. Then he would turn around and head back to repeat the process all over again.

In 1885, the railway reached Spence's Bridge and then the cattle could be driven the short distance and loaded on rail cars to be shipped by rail. But this procedure also had its difficulties. With the railway suffering its first growing pains, the schedule was far from perfect. On one occasion, McInnes held his cattle at Spence's Bridge for four days, waiting for a train that was scheduled to be there before him. On another trip, a cattle car dropped off the rails into the Fraser River, drowning 20 head of cattle.

The Triangle Ranch held the Esquimalt beef contract for six years and McInnes participated on every drive during that time. In 1889, when the contract expired, McInnes took his last drive of cattle from Kelowna to the Hamilton Corrals, then owned by the Douglas Lake Cattle Company. He stayed on as foreman of the Triangle for another four years, leaving in the spring of 1893 to get married and settle on his own place.

The railway construction boom brought with it a renewed optimism in British Columbia, and an influx of people flowed into the cities and towns of the province. As the population grew, so did the demand for beef, and ranchers all over the province responded quickly and enthusiastically. Thaddeus Harper, having lost the contract to supply beef to the railway construction crews in 1883, began to look elsewhere and found the Victoria market to be promising. An article in the Kamloops *Inland Sentinel* of December 1884 noted that Harper's cowboys had driven five bands of 100 head of cattle each from his Gang Ranch range in the Chilcotin destined for the Victoria market. All the cattle had to be swum across the Fraser River, a process that took three hours and caused the newspaper correspondent to comment, "Mr. Harper's employees deserve great praise for their skill and good management."

Winters

The life of the cowboy on the interior ranges of British Columbia was never an easy one. Climate played a crucial role in the cowboys' daily lives, whether they were feeding cattle through the long dark months of winter or herding them in the blistering summer heat. And yet, despite the hardships that took their toll on young bodies, cowboys regarded the freedom of a life open to the elements as a privilege.

However, it is a hard fact of nature that winter is essentially unpredictable. A winter that is devastating for one valley may be mild and open for the next valley over, or a late winter that sees no snow or cold by Christmas time can turn nasty and last until May. Just when a rancher felt sure that his range was secure from winter's touch, a particularly hard winter might descend without warning and wipe him out. This was frequently the case in the interior of British Columbia. In the early days, ranchers confidently believed that cattle would always be able to scratch out enough grass in the deep winter snow to keep them alive until spring. Even the hardest winters only convinced them that they needed a small haystack or two to provide feed in the harder winters. Tom Ellis, who ranched on the site of present-day Penticton, called his large haystack his "nest egg," and for most of the ranchers, that's exactly what hay represented: a safety net for the occasional cold winter. Never mind that range cattle entered the winter months rolling in fat and were turned out in the spring mostly skin and bones, it was enough that they survived the winter for the bunchgrass ranges would rejuvenate them soon enough.

The attitude in the Nicola Valley was typical of the entire area east of the coastal mountains. When ranches were established in the valley, most ranchers figured that enough of the abundant bunchgrass would stick above the snow to feed their cattle. When the severe winter of 1871–72 came and killed off a full quarter of their livestock, they dismissed it as a fluke of nature that would not be repeated for another century. By the time March brought along the first spring grass, ranchers were prepared to forget their losses and carry on. But the winter of 1879–80 was even worse. That winter, snow started falling on November 7 and continued until April. By New Year's Day of 1880, most ranchers were feeding from their meagre haystacks, and as January continued, the temperature dropped to 40 below and stayed there. More and more feed was required to keep livestock alive. When March arrived with no change in the weather, stock began to die in great numbers. Cowboys were sent out to cut brush and strip trees for feed, and some ranchers were forced to kill and burn their starving cattle. Still the snow continued to fall. It continued into the spring calving season, greatly reducing the survival rate of calves struggling in the snow and cold with only the small amount of milk their emaciated mothers could provide. By early April, more than a quarter of the cattle in the Nicola Valley lay dead in the snow, and as the warm weather slowly started to thaw things out, the sight was enough to break the hardest cowboy's heart. Carcasses were strewn from one end of the valley to the other like bodies in the aftermath of a great battle. Many ranchers sold out and left the valley, while their more optimistic colleagues swore that they would put up more hay in the future. The lesson was a hard one, but the memory of those devastated by hard winters was short. A few mild winters were enough to make most ranchers forget the hard times, and aside from adding a few hay fields to their ranches and constructing some pens for winter feeding, they worried very little about the coming winter.

The *Inland Sentinel* commented on this short-sighted attitude in an 1886 article:

WINTERING STOCK: Persons coming from the east are sometimes astonished at the way stock is kept in this country in winter when snow, as at present, is from four inches to two feet deep where drifted. Notwithstanding the recent cold spell by far the greater part of horses and cattle picked up their daily supply. Horses paw the snow to get at the grass for food and eat snow for drink; there are a large number of horses in the mountains back and to the southeast of Kamloops. Bands of cattle roam over the ranges and find sufficient, especially where the hills are bare, to retain their fat gained in the fall; numbers may be seen at times going to water holes in the ice along the river; others, we are informed, satisfy thirst with snow. Certain it is that the stock look in remarkably good condition at present. Even spring calves are running with the cattle. It is true a number of ranchers have to look after the younger portion of their bands and sometimes drive them into places prepared.

Mr. Victor Guillaume, who ranches a little east of town, has added to his former corrals and sheds extensive additions lately and his stock in this vicinity is well taken care of, while his Grande Prairie wintering ranch is all that is needed for the band kept there. It is a common thing to see parties riding over the range looking after stray cattle, which are identified by the brands and returned to their owner's ranch. Cattlemen have a good deal of anxiety respecting their stock in stormy winters, and we are pleased to be able to announce that this season has been highly favourable.[2]

This rather complacent article ran counter to the evidence of the experienced ranchers in the country. Two years earlier, the same newspaper had reported that the Okanagan had had "one of the hardest winters in 16 years. In cattle the majority of owners have lost from 10 to 12 percent and quite a number from 15 to 30 percent." The same was reported for the Nicola Valley where, it was reported, "stock have suffered severely and losses are heavy."

The extremely hard winters also took their toll on the cowboys. Frank Buckland, an early Okanagan resident, provided an eyewitness account of a bad winter in the Okanagan Valley showing just how tough it could be:

The winter of 1892–93 was extremely cold and cattlemen again suffered severe losses. Ranges and meadows were overstocked at normal times, so when a mild November and December dissolved into sub-zero temperatures at the turn of the year, the winter-feed was soon exhausted. Week after week, the wind held in the north and by March hay, at any distant haul, was selling at $100 per ton, with all the haystacks in the valley cleaned up. By April hundreds of cattle were dead from starvation and cold. Others were so weak that they had to be helped to their feet in the morning before they could feed. Cowboys, one at the horns and one at the tail, had to jump for their horses the instant a critter was helped to its feet, because these wild range cattle would attack a man on foot even if it were their last lunge.[3]

The winter of 1896 hit the area west of Kamloops most severely. Snow started to fall in October and lasted for over six months. As late as May 1, Al Fehr, who cowboyed for Johnny Wilson, reported that the snow was still 30 inches deep on the Wallachin flats and that it was possible to ride a horse over the frozen snow without breaking through. Johnny Wilson suffered particularly badly during this difficult winter, losing a huge number of cattle. The winter almost broke him, and for years afterward, he struggled to return to his earlier prosperity.

Amazingly, the ranchers still did not seem to understand that putting up winter feed was not a luxury but a necessity. As late as 1906, ranchers in the Chilcotin continued to rely on the occasional winter "chinook" to clear enough grass along the river valleys to keep the cattle alive. But the winter of 1906–07 taught them a hard lesson. Snow started falling in November and did not let up until until spring, causing thousands of head of cattle to perish in the severe weather. Even the Gang Ranch, which had owned the Harper Meadow since 1884 and occasionally hayed it, did not make an attempt to fence it for winter use until after that hard winter. Later, the Gang Ranch also strung five or six miles of split pine fence at the head of Ross Gulch to preserve the grass for winter and early spring use. Most of the other ranches in the Chilcotin finally realized the necessity of putting up extensive hay to provide for cattle through the tough winters, and from that point on, part of the summer on the ranches was devoted to haying.

Even milder winters could cause problems for the cowboys herding the cattle. Cattle tend to drift with their backs to the wind, and winter storms could move cattle great distances in the unfenced ranges of the interior. The *Vernon News* reported in January of 1892 that a large number of cattle from Spallumcheen had drifted north to Grande Prairie, where they were spotted and returned to their owners in the spring. The following year, which had one of the worst ever winters in the North Okanagan, the cattle drifted in the opposite direction. It was reported in January that "a number of cattle bearing the brands of ranchers in the Spallumcheen were brought from the Mission by Mr. John McCallum. Mac knows the brands of nearly all the breeders in the district and when cattle are gathered in for winter he sorts out the strays and restores them to their owners for a moderate fee."[4]

Moving cattle in the winter was always a challenge to the cowboys as the cattle were reluctant to move and drifting snow often obscured the trails. But extreme cold also froze rivers, which made river crossings easier as cattle could then be crossed on the ice. However, this brought its own problems. In January of 1886, Cy Hyman, one of Thaddeus Harper's cow bosses, had purchased a herd of cattle from Michael Sullivan in the Heffley Creek area. To cross them over the North Thompson River north of Kamloops, he divided them into two groups to spread the weight out. He drove the first bunch out on the ice, which appeared to be solid, and called for his cowboys to start out the second bunch. The first bunch of cattle had almost reached the edge of the river on the west side when they hit a patch of slippery ice and turned back, meeting the rest of the cattle in the middle of the river where the water was fastest. The combined weight was too much for the ice to bear and 19 head of cattle broke through. A mad scramble ensued as cowboys tried to keep the remaining cattle away from the hole as they roped and pulled out the cattle in the freezing water. Only 7 head of cattle were pulled from the water; the remaining 12 weakened and were pulled under the ice. By then, the cowboys were soaked through and cold from their endeavours, making the ride to Kamloops even more difficult.

After sitting for hours in the saddle, cowboys would often be so numbed by the cold that they would dismount and walk for a while to restore their circulation. The usual practice was to hold on to the reins in case their horse decided to head home. Sometimes the cowboy would tie the halter shank around his waist to leave his hands free so that he could slap them together and warm them up. Charlie O'Keefe, son of the well-known owner of the O'Keefe Ranch, did just that when he dismounted in cold weather. Unfortunately, slapping his hands together spooked his horse and it made a sudden jump, pulling him off his feet. He was dragged about 300 yards along a frozen trail until his brother rode up and caught the horse. By then, Charlie was nearly unconscious and was bleeding severely from being bounced along the trail. He was rushed to the local doctor, who sewed up his wounds, and within a few days Charlie was back on the job. Alas, Charlie did not appear to have learned his lesson. Some 14 years later, after driving cattle in the area southwest of Vernon, he remarked that he was too cold, because he hadn't worn his woolly chaps, and galloped on ahead of his partner, John Swan. A short while later, Swan spotted Charlie's horse without a rider and found

Charlie with his head badly cut. Apparently Charlie had flapped his arms to keep warm and spooked his horse once again, causing him to fall and trap Charlie's foot in the stirrup. This time he was not so fortunate. He never regained consciousness and died the next day.

Natural-Born Cowboys

The mystique of the cowboy spread from North America to Europe and then around the world, capturing the imaginations of young men from every corner of the globe. The ranches of the west were populated by men from every nationality imaginable, most of them fresh-faced youths. Inevitably the romance that initially attracted them wore off, as they found that the life of the cowboy ranged from mindless tedium on the cattle drives to extremes in weather that tested the spirit of even the toughest character. Only those who could withstand the gruelling way of life and enjoy the natural setting in which they found themselves were willing to stay. And so, for every young man who came to British Columbia eager for the cowboy experience, there

Okanagan rancher Val Haynes in winter. When conditions were very severe, the bandana could be pulled up over the head to cover the ears.

was one heading in the other direction who had decided that this was not the life for him. These short-term cowboys were all too common, and in later years as their memories began to blur, they would tell of their days as a cowboy with a convincing far-off look in their eyes as if it had been nothing but pure joy. And thus the mystique continued.

The others were those who found that the ranching lifestyle fit like a glove. These were the men who stayed, often drifting from ranch to ranch but always offering their best and giving full value for their wages. From among these "lifers" there rose a few who possessed that unique combination of intelligence, physical endurance and love of the cowboy way of life. These were the crème de la crème, the best of all those who chose the cowboy profession. They were the ones who stood out in a crowd and who were chosen by the owners of the large ranches to manage some important aspect of the operation. They were the "natural-born cowboys."

Newman Squires: King of the Range

Newman Squires was born in the eastern United States in 1839 but, at the age of nine, moved to California with his parents. Sometime after that, he was orphaned and went to live with neighbours on a stock ranch. There he learned the cattle business and developed the skills that would stand him in such good stead in the years to come. In his early twenties, Squires joined Jerome Harper in driving cattle from California to British Columbia. Thanks to his abilities and character he soon took charge of the British Columbia end of the Harper drives, meeting the drive of about 500 head of cattle at Osoyoos Lake and making sure that they arrived at the Cariboo market in good shape. During the height of the gold rush years, he oversaw three drives a year of cattle, horses and milk cows, all for sale. The season usually ended at the beginning of November, after which Squires would winter at the Harper Ranch west of Fort Kamloops.

Squires was an expert at roping or horse breaking and always rode the finest and best-trained horses. A deadly shot with the Colt revolver, those who knew him said that it was "head or no chicken" with him at 25 paces. He was also a man of sterling character, honest and quiet about his own abilities. He never drank or used tobacco in any form and, unlike the average cowboy, was never known to use profanity of any sort. He was a big, good-looking man in his prime who was liked by everyone who knew him and was a born leader of men.

When the decline of the gold rush activity brought a halt to the cattle drives to British Columbia, Squires looked after the Harper cattle interests at the Harper Ranch and, later, at the Gang Ranch in the Chilcotin. He was in charge of the great Harper drive from the Chilcotin in 1876 that ended up in San Francisco two years later, and on this and other drives, he showed an incredible memory for the cattle in his care. After a few days on the trail he would have all the cattle fixed in his mind. They would always be kept under night guard and counted every morning. Squires and one of his cowboys would take their places about 30 yards apart and let the stock drift through to get a correct count. If two or three had strayed off during the night, he would describe them in detail. The cowboys would shake their heads in disbelief, but sure enough, when the cattle were found, Squires's description was inevitably correct.

Thaddeus Harper came to trust Squires completely when it came to handling stock and put him in charge of stock operations at the Gang Ranch. In 1884, Squires drove 200 head of horses for Harper from here through the Okanagan all the way to the Fort McLeod area in what is now southern Alberta. Squires left in April and was back in the Kamloops area by the end of November.

Squires married a Shuswap Native woman, Sophie. They had two children, Lucinda and Charles, and eventually purchased a ranch at Copper Creek where Squires raised his own cattle and kept a few racehorses. Like most of the men who had been in British Columbia during the gold rush, he dabbled in mining, having an interest in several copper claims near his ranch.

His son, Charlie, served in the Boer War with Lord Strathcona's Horse and then returned to North America. A born horseman like his father, he travelled with Buffalo Bill's Wild West Show for several years before settling on a ranch near Calgary.

Newman Squires died from heart trouble in November of 1898 at the age of 59. His funeral was widely attended, and he was buried in the Kamloops cemetery. His obituary in the November 29, 1898, Kamloops *Inland Sentinel* was accompanied by a poem that was signed simply "D."

NEWMAN SQUIRES
Hang the saddle up, tie the lariat on, the rider's day is past and o'er;
Turn the old horse loose on the range to feed, thro' day and night for evermore;
The snow lies light on the hill tops white, drapes the pinetrees, drapes the plains;
Nature weeps and supplies a shroud for the old time King of Rope and Range.

Never again shall the untamed steed feel the master's hand and the master know
Never again shall the rope fly swift from the master's hand with his one sure throw;
Never again shall the driven steer hear the master's voice on the overland trail.
Never again shall the wild range see his form 'neath the sun or the moonlight pale.

Oh! Newman Squires, when the canting friars have lost their jobs and God puts men true,
True to the best that exists in man, to corral the sinners, He'll call on you.
Oh! Newman Squires, God speed you well, o'er the narrow trail that all must go;
At peace with God, at peace with men, 'neath the green turf sod in peace lie low.

Joe Payne

When J.B. Greaves was setting up the Douglas Lake Cattle Ranch in the early 1880s, he realized he needed a top-notch cow boss to tend the cattle while he looked after the business end of things. He was fortunate to hire Joe Payne, an American with rich and varied experience in handling cattle. Payne followed closely the practices that Greaves had established at the Douglas Lake Ranch and remained as cow boss for about 10 years. During that time he married Matilda Genelle, who was born in Ontario of French Canadian parentage and had recently arrived in the area. Because of the rough state of living accommodations at Douglas Lake, Matilda lived in Kamloops, and Payne visited her on his frequent trips to Kamloops with cattle for shipping.

Payne was a natural at handling cattle and men. Under his management, the Douglas Lake herd thrived and the cowboys who worked for him developed into an efficient crew. The Native cowboys worked particularly well with Payne, who had the patience to show them the preferred methods of handling cattle. He conscientiously divided his huge herd into small groups and moved them carefully throughout the year to avoid overgrazing of the precious bunchgrass. His techniques for getting cattle out of the bush, driving, sorting and holding cattle for market and weaning became standard practice for decades to come. Payne was also an excellent veterinarian, and under his care, few cattle were lost in calving or to sickness.

In the late 1890s, Payne left the Douglas Lake Ranch and went to work as a cattle buyer for Malcolm McInnes, a former Nicola Valley cattleman, who, in partnership with Pat Burns, was supplying huge amounts of beef to the mining centres of the Kootenays. Payne was responsible for buying cattle in the B.C. interior and driving them to points where they could be shipped to the Kootenays. In 1897, when the Klondike gold rush started, Payne rounded up cattle from the Cariboo, Chilcotin and Thompson areas for Burns and Company and assembled them at the Gang Ranch. From there they were driven to Ashcroft and shipped by rail to the coast and by barge up to Skagway. Payne and his cowboys then drove the cattle over the White Pass and overland 40 miles to Lake Bennett. There the cattle were loaded on scows to be shipped across Lake Bennett, then through a series of lakes and rivers to the Yukon River where they travelled an additional 200 miles to Dawson. The cattle sold at Dawson for a dollar a pound or $800 to $1000 per head alive.[5] This was the first of a succession of cattle drives that Burns and Company organized to the Klondike from the B.C. interior.

Payne worked for Pat Burns for the next 10 or 12 years as a cattle buyer and trusted agent. In 1911, Burns sent him to Mexico to check out land for possible purchase to add to Burns's expanding empire. This was not a simple mission. Payne had to remain inconspicuous and not reveal that the millionaire Burns was behind the purchase. As well, the political situation in Mexico was far from stable, with revolutionaries like Pancho Villa leading the opposition to the government. Never the most respectable-looking person at the best of times, Payne was arrested by the Mexican authorities and put in jail. It was some time before Burns and Company, working with the Canadian government, could convince the Mexican authorities that Payne's activities were legitimate.

Sometime during the First World War, Payne retired from the cattle business and went into partnership with Fred Bradley to operate the Brunswick Billiard Parlour on Victoria Street in Kamloops. But his restless nature and ill health soon prompted him to accept an offer from Dr. Vereerbrughen of Kamloops to go ranching in Argentina. From Argentina he relocated to Brazil and finally, in 1924, he moved to California. He died there two years later, mourned by all the old-time cowboys who knew him as one of the best.

Tools of the Trade

By the middle of the 1870s, the term "cowboy" was being used to describe the young mounted riders driving cattle out of Texas. This term was originally used east of the Rocky Mountains, the preferred term on the other side of the Great Divide being "buckaroo." But this did not last for long. By the early 1880s, bolstered by the mostly mythical image of the "wild west" portrayed in dime novels, the love affair between the general public of North America and Europe and the "cowboy" had begun. Soon the young men involved in British Columbia ranching abandoned the terms "drover" and "buckaroo" and happily accepted the title "cowboy." With this new title came a gradual acceptance of the "uniform" that came with the image. The cowboy of British Columbia never looked back.

Unquestionably, the most identifiable aspect of the cowboy's uniform was his horse. Early cowboy Joe Mora wrote that, dismounted, the cowboy was "just a plain bowlegged human who smelled very horsey at times, slept in his underwear and was subject to boils and dyspepsia."[6] The horse allowed him to cover great distances in search of strayed cattle, and the size of the horse was enough to strike fear in the heart of the meanest long-horned steer. Normally the mounts that a cowboy used were supplied by the ranch he worked for, meaning that few cowboys actually owned a horse. Given the fact that the earliest horses in British Columbia were small strong cayuses that were descended from the wild horses of the northwest and were capable of only a few hours of hard riding, it was usual for a cowboy to have several horses at his disposal. The relationship between the cowboy and his horse was always a practical working arrangement, with the cowboy feeding and caring for the horse in return for the often hard riding required for his work. It was not unusual for a horse to be burned out after seven years of gruelling work. Nonetheless, the horse became a significant element in the self-image of the cowboy and remains so to this day.

When he was fully outfitted for his job, the cowboy was covered from head to foot in protective gear that identified him as distinctively as a knight's armour identified its owner. Each item that he used had a definite purpose and put together formed his "tools of the trade." From the wide-brimmed hat that protected him from the scorching sun of the B.C. interior to the high-heeled boots, the cowboy's gear was designed for a purpose. This did not mean that the beauty of a well-tooled saddle or a colourful silk neckerchief did not enter into the selection of the item. But everything a cowboy used for his job was functional. These tools of the trade were common to all who identified themselves as cowboys.

Saddles

The first saddles to arrive in North America were primarily Spanish war saddles with high cantles, to keep the rider from being driven over the back of his horse, and high forks to protect the rider in front. Once the Spanish established their dominance over the native people of Central America, their attention shifted to development of the resources in the new land, and the raising of cattle became a major industry. The Mexican *vaqueros* found that the war saddle was not suited for working cattle in the wide open spaces of Mexico. They therefore developed a lighter saddle consisting only of a hide-covered tree with a rather low cantle and a short fork with no saddle horn. When a cow was roped, it was secured to the horse's tail. Not surprisingly, this was not entirely satisfactory, and by 1830 Mexican *vaqueros* had developed a saddle with a saddle horn on which to attach a rope. Thus originated the stock saddle in North America.

The early stock saddles were covered with a removable leather sheet called a *mochila*, which had slits cut in it through which the cantle and fork of the saddle protruded. Californian saddles tended to have a small horn with a small flat cap, while the Texas saddles, especially what was called the Hope saddle, had large flat horn caps. This difference arose because the roping techniques of the California *vaqueros* differed from their Texas counterparts. The *Californianos* wrapped their braided rawhide *reatas* around the saddle horn, allowing the roper to vary the tension on the rope and save wear and tear on the saddle. The Texas cowboys preferred to tie their ropes to the

Barkerville street scene in 1869. The horse on the left has a "California" saddle, complete with *tapaderos*, and the horse on the right has a saddle from which the *mochila* has been removed.

saddle horn, and the resulting shock of a 1,500-pound bull hitting the end of their rope required a much thicker, sturdier horn. California saddles tended to be more ornate than their Texas cousins with carved leather and metal *conchos*.

It was this California-style saddle that found its way north to the valleys of western Oregon and eventually to British Columbia during the gold-rush years. For the British, being used to their own style of saddle, this strange aberration was a "Mexican saddle." Whatever its local name, the California stock saddle was everywhere and was used by drovers and miners alike. Photographs of the main street of Barkerville in the 1860s show the widespread use of the California saddle with the characteristic saddle horn and cantle. Most have saddle horns that are wrapped around the neck but with uncovered caps; some of the saddles have *tapaderos* over the stirrups; and all appear to be "centre fire" rigged, having a single cinch located midway on the saddle.

Whips

Although the Spanish *vaquero* brought most of the tools of the cattle trade to the grasslands west of the Rocky Mountains, there were some items that found their origins not in the salt marshes of southwestern Spain but in the highlands of Great Britain. In Britain the cattle herders, mostly women and children on foot, controlled their cattle with long whips, called "bullwhips." These whips were braided out of rawhide or tanned leather, and it was claimed that a good bullwhip-wielding man could control a hundred head of cattle.

It is not surprising then that the introduction of British breeds of cattle into Jamaica and later South Carolina in the late 1600s saw the use of the cattle whip as the main cattle control device. In fact, the widespread use of the bullwhip gave the cowboys of the Carolinas and Florida their distinctive name, "crackers," after the sound of the bullwhip that was used to manage cattle. Cattle were not beaten by the whips but were controlled by the sound of the cracking of the whip beside their heads. The "crackers" became expert whip users, and on the cattle trails and grasslands of the east, the whip became the main tool of the cowboy.

The spread of cattle into the mid-west and eventually over the Oregon Trail to the area west of the Rockies also introduced the bullwhip, which proved to be indispensable in the tighter confines of the wooded valleys of Oregon and Washington. Many drovers who pushed cattle into British Columbia in the 1860s were from families who had come from the mid-west over the Oregon Trail and they were familiar with the use of the bullwhip. Myron Brown was one of these and in his diary frequently records "mending my whip" or "braiding a new whip," indicating how useful the bullwhip was in driving cattle.

The other type of whip used by the British Columbia cowboys was the quirt, a short flexible woven-leather whip. It was made with a handle about a foot long and two to four heavy loose lashes hanging from one end and the other end with a loop to hang around the cowboy's wrist or saddlehorn. The word is derived from the Spanish *cuarta de cordon* meaning "whip of cord." Unlike the bullwhip, this type of whip was brought north from Mexico. The flexible handles of most quirts were loaded with shot or lead to give them weight. Some quirts were made with stiff handles because they were easier to handle. The quirt was used to strike down rearing horses that threatened to fall backwards or to make a horse increase its speed.

Ropes

A rope may look like a simple thing, but next to a horse, it was the most important tool of the early cowboy and continues to be an indispensable part of the cattle trade. Roping has always been the only way to catch and hold cattle and horses and the only way to throw an animal for branding or doctoring. In the hands of a competent cowboy, roping can be a skill that borders on art; it was the most difficult of all cowboy skills and an expert roper spent most of his working life practising and perfecting his technique.

The braided rawhide rope, referred to as *la reata*, came to Mexico from the south of Spain with the first Spanish-speaking *vaqueros*. From Mexico, the use of the rope spread to California where it became one of the most important tools for handling cattle from horseback. The old-time *Californianos* became masters of *la reata larga*, a rawhide rope up to 100 feet long, and this skill passed on to the English-speaking cowboys of California, Nevada and Oregon. From there the use of the braided rawhide rope travelled to British Columbia with the Mexican packers and other cowboys.

The *reata* was made of thin strands of rawhide cut from green cow or buffalo hides. Four, six and eight plaits (strands) were used in braiding the ropes and good *reateros* (rope makers) were in great demand. Unfortunately there were few good *reata* builders, and although the *reata* was an excellent rope that held its loop very well, it was soon replaced in British Columbia with a twisted rope made from vegetable fibre. This latter type of rope was cheaper and easier to make and, if well made, was stronger and had a smoother running surface. The twisted fibre rope tended to be much shorter, averaging about 40 feet in length. Its Spanish name, *la reata*, soon became anglicized as "lariat."

The braided rawhide *reata* continued to be used in California, Nevada and Oregon and, to a limited extent, in British Columbia. In the hands of a Mexican *vaquero* it was a formidable tool. As a rawhide rope is too stiff to tie hard and fast to a saddle horn and does not stand up well against the weight of a roped steer, the *vaqueros* used the technique of wrapping the rope around the saddle horn. The Spanish term "*dar la vuelta*," meaning literally "to give it the turn" or to "give a twist" became corrupted by the English-speaking cowboys to "dally-welta" or just plain "dally." One of the true distinctions of the cowboys west of the Rocky Mountains was their technique of dallying the rope as opposed to cowboys east of the Rockies who preferred to tie their ropes to the saddle horn. Dallying a rope is easier on the stock being roped and on the saddle horse, as it eliminates the sudden jerk when the animal reaches the end of the rope. As well, in the case of an accident, the dallied rope is easier to slip off the horn.

The Mexican *vaqueros* and packers brought with them to British Columbia a strong rope constructed from the fibre of the maguey plant (from which the popular Mexican drink "mescal" is also produced). The Mexican maguey rope was a four-strand rope only 3/8 inch thick and came in lengths from 35 up to 75 feet or even more. The maguey fibre is extra hard so that it holds a wide loop and can be thrown very fast, but it stiffens in damp weather and breaks very easily if tied hard and fast. Still, *vaqueros* and cowboys in the dry interior of British Columbia preferred the maguey and used it whenever it was available. The maguey fibre's Mexican cousin was sisal, which was produced from the leaves of the Agave cactus plant. Like the maguey, sisal

has a hard fibre, but like cotton ropes, sisal was too soft and never became popular with the old-time cowboys.

The most popular and common rope of the early days was made of manilla hemp, constructed of three strands twisted extra hard for strength and smoothness. Even though it was not true hemp, being produced from a variety of the wild banana plant, rope makers in North America recognized its superior qualities even before the American Civil War. Soon it was the fibre rope of choice among the cowboys of the west, arriving in British Columbia with the early drovers. The major supplier of manilla hemp ropes was the Plymouth Cordage Company in Massachusetts that produced a strong three-strand rope that became the favourite of British Columbia cowboys. It was not uncommon for large ranches to buy large rolls of manilla hemp rope from which cowboys could cut the length of their choice.

Until a manilla rope is limbered up, it will neither throw nor coil well. Most cowboys stretched their ropes to remove the kinks and render them pliable. Sometimes the cowboy would stretch it between two trees or fence posts. Another popular technique was for two cowboys to tie their new ropes to each other's saddle horns and back their horses up slowly to stretch their ropes. Once stretched, ropes were often conditioned with tallow or soaked in linseed oil to waterproof them and to keep them pliable. Some cowboys, however, found this made a rope too greasy to handle and easily discoloured from dirt, and preferred to leave their rope untouched. When a rope became limp and lifeless from hard use, it was discarded and a new rope either cut from the roll at the ranch or purchased from the nearest supplier.

The "honda" (from the Spanish *hondo* or "eye") was the eyelet in the loop end of the rope through which the main line of the rope passed to form a loop. Hondas were most often tied in the end of the rope with a small piece of leather sewn on the upper end of the loop to keep the rope from burning through during rough work. In the early days, oval metal hondas were popular for a brief time but they were difficult to splice into the end of the rope and were found to be too free running and too heavy to hold a loop. They also had a tendency to injure the eye of the animal being roped.

Another type of rope brought to British Columbia by the Mexicans was the *mecate* or braided hair rope. These were usually made from horsehair from the mane or tail (mane hair was softer and silkier than the tail hair) and were about an inch in diameter. *Mecates* were never used for roping purposes, but because the different colours of horsehair made for beautiful

Cowboy with braided rawhide *reata*. Rawhide ropes were stiff and held their loop very well, so they could be thrown accurately for a great distance.

Cowboys stretching their ropes. It was a common practice to play "tug-o-war" with manilla ropes to make them softer and more flexible and to train horses to keep pressure on the rope.

designs, they became popular as tie ropes on hackamores, halters and reins where a short rope was useful. They were also used by some horse trainers when breaking colts—the stiff hair ends against the colt's neck made it aware of the pressure and it therefore responded quicker.

Chaps

Spanish influence pervades the vocabulary of the cowboy so it is not surprising to learn that the word "chaps" comes from the Spanish *chaparreras* meaning "leg armour." The use of chaps for leg protection can be traced back to the Pacific coastal areas of Mexico where brush and thorns were common. *Vaqueros* developed *armas*, a slab of cowhide hung over the pommel of the saddle to protect the rider's legs and the horse's breast from injury. As the cattle culture spread into southern California, the *vaqueros* found that the country was more open and so adapted the *armas* to a smaller, lighter deerskin that was fastened around the rider's belt and reached below the knee, where it was held in place by tie-strings. These lighter, more flexible coverings, referred to as *armitas,* protected the legs and clothes and were cooler in the summer.

The California *armitas* eventually came to be called *chaparreras* and were quickly adopted by the English-speaking cowboys of California. From there they spread with the Spanish cattle into Oregon where they proved very useful in the sagebrush country of the interior. Their name was soon shortened to "chaps," and some of the early drovers into British Columbia wore them for protection from the brush and thorns found along the narrow trails.

The earliest chaps in British Columbia were a closed-leg chap consisting of two long tubes of leather, into which the legs were stuck, joined into a belt at the waist. The seam was sewn on the outside of each leg with enough leather left to be cut into a fringe, an adaptation that seems to have been borrowed from the Native legging. The way the two legs tapered down to the ankle reminded the drovers of the two barrels of a shotgun with a choke at the muzzle, so they called them "shotgun chaps."

Shotgun chaps were light, warm and water-resistant to a certain extent. But the cowboys found that oiling the chaps to make them more waterproof also made them stiff and uncomfortable in cold weather, so they started covering them with pelts of various kinds to provide more warmth in cold weather and more water resistance. Soon the chaps themselves were made of the pelts from bear, goat, deer and other animals with the hair left on the outside. These "woollies," as they were called, became very popular in the harsh northern climate of British Columbia. They also offered protection from bruises when a rider was thrown against a fence or tree by a mean horse. By the turn of the century, cowboys in B.C. almost universally wore "woollies," most often made from long, thick-haired Angora goatskins.

Cowboys ready to rope horses. The cowboy on the left has "shotgun" chaps, which effectively protected the legs but were extremely difficult to put on and take off.

The main drawback to shotgun chaps and woollies was the difficulty in getting them on and off. Since they were tight to the leg, they had to be pulled on over sock feet before the boots and spurs were put on. This was awkward and time consuming. Soon a chap was developed that buckled over the legs with snaps, so the cowboy could simply fasten the belt and then reach down and snap the legs in place. This design allowed for a flap of leather to extend beyond the side of the legs much like wings hanging back from the legs. As this flap became more pronounced, the particular style came to be known as "bat wing" chaps. The plain leather surface could be decorated with silver conchos and leather tooling or overlays, making for a very fancy design. A type of bat wing chap was developed in Wyoming with a wing that was narrower and straight, the underpart of the leg being cut back to the knee. This particular cut of chap was called a "Cheyenne leg."

In the hotter southern areas of the United States, a variation of the early *armitas* was developed, which consisted of a chap that only extended down past the knee. These short, fringed chaps, called "chinks" from the Spanish *chinquederos,* were seldom found in British Columbia in the early days.

The earliest chaps buckled at the back and were laced together at the front. The straight belt with a full lace front proved dangerous if a rider was pitched forward on the saddle horn. If he was hung up, it was very difficult to extract himself. Over the years the lacing at the front became less and less and chaps were designed with a distinct dip in the front centre. In more recent times the two sides of the chap were joined by a single thin lace, which would break easily if the rider was hung up.

Boots

From the days of the Mongols, who swept through eastern Europe on horseback wearing boots with high red wooden heels, horsemen have preferred a high leather boot with an elevated heel that allows them to place their foot securely in the stirrup. In fact, in European society of the 1600s, the distinctive riding boot became a sign of nobility. Owning and caring for a horse required significant wealth and placed a person above the common man, so riders with high heels and knee-high leather boots became associated with the upper classes. To this day, we refer to someone who is wealthy or aristocratic as "well heeled."

The cavaliers of Stuart England who immigrated to the American south brought with them the high-heeled leather boots that indicated their class. By

The white angora goatskin "woollies" this cowboy is wearing were good at shedding water and were warm in cold weather.

the early 1800s, the boots, which were shortened to just cover the calf, were named in honour of Arthur Wellsley, First Duke of Wellington, the victor at the Battle of Waterloo in 1815. During the American Civil War, all military officers and cavalry wore a "Full Wellington," a two-piece leather boot. After the war, the tens of thousands of surplus boots were sold to horsemen, especially in the west, and the Wellington became the standard boot for all western horsemen. The Coffeyville pattern, as it was called, had a higher Cuban heel than the regular military version and was favoured by the early drovers who preferred a heel that they could brace against the stirrup when holding a taut rope. These boots travelled to British Columbia during the gold-rush years with the drovers and the California miners and soon became the standard footwear.

In the late 1870s, a bootmaker named H.J. Justin of Spanish Fort, on the Red River in north Texas, modified the Full Wellington on the advice of the trail drivers to produce more of a pointed-toe boot that could be easily inserted into the stirrup. He also inserted a steel-shank arch for more riding support. The popularity of this modified boot spread rapidly throughout the west and arrived in British Columbia by the 1880s. By that time, the cowboy boot had become a separate style with elaborate stitch patterns on the sides for more support and stovepipe tops. These boots came in two basic designs:

Okanagan cowboys doctoring a calf. Note the different types of boots. The cowboy in the middle has a low-heeled lace-up boot, while the other two have high Wellington-type boots with Cuban heels.

the Full Wellington, which consisted of two pieces, a front and a back, and the Dress Wellington, which consisted of a vamp (front of foot), a counter cover (to cover the heel) and front and back tops.

. Lace-up boots were also very common in the British Columbia ranching frontier. Many cowboys preferred the extra support that laces provided and early photographs show the high-heeled lace-up to be popular. Lace-ups were also easier to remove when they were wet. Leather contracts when it is wet and the pull-on type of boot was almost impossible to remove. Cowboys used laundry soap and flour to dust the inside of these boots to make them easier to take off, but despite the inconvenience, tight boots remained the order of the day.

The high heel remained popular on the cowboy boot, because it prevented the foot from going through the stirrup and catching in such a way that the rider could be dragged by a runaway horse. Early cowboys always "homed" their foot in the stirrup, with the boots far enough into the stirrup to have the boot heels resting against the stirrup. They maintained that it was less tiring to ride this way but it was also more difficult to extract the boot in times of trouble. The high-heeled boot was also good for digging in when the cowboy was roping on foot. The practical value of a high heel is certainly significant, but the added height that it gave to the cowboy should not be discounted. In some ways, the cowboys were not much different from the Mongols and the cavaliers.

Clothing

The most distinctive articles of cowboy apparel were wide-brimmed hats, high-heeled boots and leather or woolly chaps. All of these were designed for a purpose, and as is often the case with what we wear, they made a fashion statement as well. But there were many other articles of clothing that were standard for cowboys. Some were chosen for their serviceability and differed little from the clothing worn by most farm labourers of the time. We can get a glimpse of the working cowboy attire at the turn of the 20th century in a letter written to a young Englishman, Brian Kesteven de Peyster Chance, from a former Douglas Lake Ranch cowboy, Frank Newstand. Chance was heading to British Columbia to work on the Douglas Lake Ranch and had asked Newstand for his advice on a number of matters, including what clothing to wear, to which Newstand replied:

> Now as to clothing, in the summer blue jean overalls purchased at one dollar and a quarter at the Ranche store with a cotton shirt will fill the bill; but for autumn and winter, let me most strongly recommend the best quality and warmest underclothes, vest and drawers I found layers invaluable then good

flannel shirts with ditto collars. Old fashioned velvet corduroy breeches or I prefer trousers made fairly to fit from the knees down as riding boots are distinctly cold in winter and if you get a job riding you will try a pair of chaps, and these will pull over tight trousers and you can wear either riding boots or what I prefer to ride in during zero weather, ordinary walking boots and overshoes over them … Have a good coat and waistcoat of whipcord for winter and for the rest all the old clothes you have by you. Remember, decent underclothing, flannel shirts and boots cannot be bought in Canada, most other things are obtainable … I think a small strong trunk with a good lock the best thing for your kit; things might be stolen from a kit-bag; if riding, one is often away from the bunk house for a week[7]

Newstand went on to mention that "there are plenty of good fellows in a Douglas Lake haying gang that will help a fellow along if he wants help but don't begin to tell them 'how they do things in England.' This is fatal." The young Chance must have heeded Newstand's advice well—he remained at the Douglas Lake Ranch for the next 42 years and was manager from 1940 until 1967.

Because of the inevitable wear and tear that cowboy clothing was subjected to, everything was made of the best material and therefore cost more than the average price for clothing. Pure wool and cotton were the order of the day, and clothing was purchased large to allow for freedom of action. Pant

Group of Similkameen Native cowboys wearing woollies chaps, beaded gauntlets, roping cuffs, neckerchiefs, vests and the ubiquitous cowboy hat.

legs were wide and long to allow the pants to ride up easily when a cowboy was in the saddle, which was most of the time. Levi Strauss denim jeans were popular throughout the ranching country as were heavy duck canvas pants. Cotton shirts in the summer and plaid wool shirts in the winter were standard wear, and since early shirts did not come with pockets, a vest was generally worn, both for extra warmth and to supply pockets for the cowboy's "makins" (tobacco and papers) and personal items. In the summertime in British Columbia, cowboys always carried a rain slicker, made large enough to cover the entire body and legs and open up the back to fit over the horse and saddle.

Gloves too were standard wear for the working cowboys of British Columbia, especially when working in the brush or when dallying their ropes. Gauntlet gloves were especially popular, and the Native cowboys proudly wore beautifully beaded gauntlets made by their mothers or wives. If they did not have gauntlets to cover their wrists, cowboys wore leather cuffs that laced or buckled up over their wrists. Leather cuffs usually had ornate stamping on them, purely for decorative purposes, reflecting the cowboys' surprisingly un-macho attitude that pretty worked every bit as well as plain.

This attitude of combining utility and appearance was particularly evident when it came to neck coverings. Cowboys wore neckerchiefs around their necks to pull up over the mouth when following cattle over dusty trails. Neckerchiefs were also used for warmth in the winter months and, in the coldest weather, could be tied around a rider's head to protect his ears from freezing. Silk proved to be the most effective for neckerchiefs because it kept the dust out more effectively than cotton, and it kept the heat in during the winter. The cowboy's "glad rag," as the neckerchief was affectionately called, was an indispensable part of his attire.

Given the pragmatism of the cowboy's clothes, it is perhaps not surprising that the cowboy style of dress has changed very little from the earliest days of the open range. Today's cowboy could easily be mistaken for his counterpart of 100 years ago, proving that the tried and true clothing and gear will always be a part of cowboy tradition.

Chapter Four

THE OPEN RANGE ERA

The Mining Hoax That Wasn't

It was a sweltering hot day in the summer of 1884. The heat seemed to bring everything to a standstill, with humans and animals all seeking out the shade. On the Allisons' ranch near Princeton the cattle were all on summer range, and aside from a few cowboys looking out for sick or mud-bogged cattle, the ranch hands were free until haying season. Three of the Allison cowboys, Bill McKeon, Billy Elwell and Harry Hobbes, drew their wages and dressed themselves in their finest for a visit to the nearby town of Oroville, just across the border. Susan Allison described these cowboys as "three of the best and most cheerful perverters of the truth I ever knew." Their talents for storytelling were no doubt enhanced by their intake of strong beverages, and their visit "to town" was to prove the spark that ignited a gold rush unlike anything British Columbia had seen in a long time.

The cowboys' week of celebration in Oroville was everything they hoped it would be. The three returned to the ranch with empty pockets and aching heads, but with a twinkle in their bloodshot eyes, they told anyone who would listen that life in the Princeton area would not remain dull for long. Sure enough, the next day a group of miners arrived in the area, asking about the "new strike." The miners had seen gold dust that the cowboys had brought to Oroville and that they had boasted had come from a new gold creek. Now, the Similkameen River had been producing fine gold in small quantities for the previous 20 years, but there was certainly no "new strike" that anyone knew about. The cowboys who created the story were, needless to say, reluctant to give any details about their "find," since it was based primarily on hot air and whisky. Nonetheless, the miners decided to try the surrounding creeks and actually managed to find a fairly

Hans Richter wearing typical cowboy attire of the early 1900s and holding a manilla hemp rope.

rich sandbar in the Similkameen River. However, it was nothing to get too excited about.

Most of the miners were hard workers, but one of their number, Johnny Chance, was too lazy to put in a good day's work, so he was relegated to the role of cook. Ironically, his idleness would work, to the advantage of disgruntled colleagues. Susan Allison wrote that:

> They made him cook but as the weather grew hotter that was too much exertion for him, so his partners gave him a gun and told him to get them a few grouse. He departed and strolled about till near sunset he found a nice cool creek that emptied itself into the river. Here he threw himself down hill with his feet paddling the cool water, when a ray of light fell on something yellow. He drew it towards him, picked it up and found it was a nugget of pure gold. He looked into the water again and there was another, then another. He pulled out his buckskin purse and slowly filled it, then picking up his gun he strolled back to camp where he became a hero and the discoverer of Granite Creek.[1]

Word of the discovery soon leaked out to the outside world, and the Granite Creek rush began in earnest early in 1885. Gold seekers crowded over the Hope Mountains with toboggans and snowshoes, and, true to the cowboys' prediction, life soon perked up in the Princeton area. By mid-1885, Granite Creek had more than 700 miners working a five-mile stretch of creek, and a town with seven stores, two restaurants, two saloons and a butcher shop sprang up at the mouth of the creek.

In a province founded on mining excitement, it is not surprising that every cowboy kept an eye out for gold or other minerals that might catapult him from working cowboy to ranch owner in one fell swoop. Mere rumours of gold were enough to make entire towns drop everything and head out to the hills with gold pan and shovel to try their luck. C.W. Holliday, an early resident of Vernon, recalled:

> So we all dreamed gold, and mining was almost the only topic of conversation; we formed mining companies and gambled ridiculously in their shares; one enthusiastic individual even opened a mining exchange in an empty store, with a big black board on which he chalked up the latest quotations on the stock of mines which only existed in the promoters' imaginations. We all carried around chunks of rock in our pockets which we would fish out and show to anyone who would look at them and we would talk learnedly of geology and petrology of which we knew nothing ... I am sure all of the range land within easy reach of Vernon was staked out ... I knew a few

men who were bush ranching at that time whose cabins happened to be conveniently situated just at the foot of a steep hill; they started tunneling right at their back door so that they could be handy to their work; it added a pleasant variation to their usual occupation, and a tunnel was a nice cool place to work in on a hot day, and as one of them remarked, his mine would make a dandy roothouse.[2]

Among the many mining "excitements" over the years, one of the most enduring and beneficial to the struggling British Columbia economy focused attention on the West Kootenays. Prospectors had been aware of the potential of the Kootenays for hard-rock mining since the gold-rush days of the 1860s, but it was the early 1880s before they began to find paying quantities of precious minerals. In 1882, the Blue Bell silver–lead mine was discovered on the Riondel peninsula on Kootenay Lake and, in later years, silver–lead and zinc were discovered in the Slocan, coal in the East Kootenays, copper near Phoenix and lode gold farther west at Camp McKinney, Fairview and Hedley. At first, only the American miners from Montana, Idaho and Washington showed any interest in the West Kootenays, but in 1895 a sharp rise in the price of silver brought prospectors from all over the world to the area. Nelson, originally laid out by Gilbert Malcolm Sproat in 1887, prospered as capital poured into the Silver King mine. The great West Kootenay boom, which started in earnest in 1896, soon made the area world famous. The mining towns of Rossland, Sandon, Grand Forks, Greenwood, Trail and Phoenix sprang up to meet the needs of the miners.

All this excitement attracted the attention of Alberta butcher/entrepreneur Pat Burns, who was busy establishing butcher shops throughout the west. In 1893, he arranged a partnership with Malcolm McInnes, who had ranched in the Nicola Valley and was among the first to drive horses across the mountains to the prairies in 1882. Burns and McInnes entered into the butcher business in a big way in the Kootenays, agreeing that McInnes would focus on the East Kootenays, and Burns on the West Kootenays. Burns established shops in Nelson, Kaslo, Sandon and Three Forks, all in 1893, and in Rossland and the Boundary country a few years later. Initially, Burns shipped most of his cattle from Alberta to the Kootenays. In June of 1893, for example, he shipped 14 cars of cattle to Golden on the CPR and then had them driven south through the East Kootenays and over the mountains to Three Forks. However, the process took 25 days and was very expensive.

Burns turned his attention to the cattle ranges of the South Okanagan and the Similkameen as a much more reliable and cost-efficient source of cattle. The Dewdney Trail from Osoyoos to Fort Steele had long been used as an east-west corridor and, in the 1880s, had been successfully used to drive cattle east to the Crowsnest Pass and onto the prairies. Jim McConnell, who had been driving J.C. Haynes's cattle over the trail to winter on the lush grazing lands on the open ranges of the Kettle River for years, established a ranch at Grand Forks in 1882. The Dewdney Trail offered the best route into the Kootenay mining areas, and Burns let the cattlemen of the South Okanagan and Similkameen know that he would purchase any and all cattle that they could bring him. The ranchers were happy to oblige. For years they had been driving their cattle over the western section of the trail to Hope, where the cattle could be sold to the butchers who owned shops at the coast, but the western part of the Dewdney Trail was only open from the middle

of June until the middle of November. From Osoyoos east, it was open for a longer period.

Thousands of head of cattle were driven over the trail from the stock ranches of Frank Richter, John F. Allison, Manuel Barcelo, Dick Cawston and W.H. Lowe in the Similkameen; J.C. Haynes and Tom Ellis in the South Okanagan; and J.R. Jackson, the Bubar brothers, Allen Eddy, C. Carlton and E.M. Cudworth in the Boundary country. During the mining boom, the drives averaged 100 head of cattle once a month during the summer and early fall and 250 head in the last drive of the season during the late fall or early winter. The drives were, as always, conducted at a leisurely pace so that the cattle could graze along the way, and the usual day's drive covered about 10 miles. Even in those days, the cattle were a mixed variety. More and more white-faced Herefords appeared in the South Okanagan, but Shorthorns, mostly of a roan colour, predominated, with a few Aberdeen Angus or Galloways in the mix.

The drives were colourful processions with the cowboys wearing the clothing that had now become a symbol of their trade. Every cowboy had high-heeled riding boots, a large Stetson hat and a brightly coloured neckerchief around his neck. The Native cowboys inevitably sported beautiful beaded gauntlets and fringed buckskin jackets adorned with fine beadwork. Angora goatskin chaps came into fashion by the turn of the century and replaced the heavy leather chaps of the earlier years. Cowboys sat atop high-quality saddles made by the interior's excellent saddle-makers and rode the swift, hardy mountain ponies that lived wild in the surrounding mountainous country.

Two Native cowboys on the Haynes Ranch near Osooyos. By the late 1800s, the clothing and gear of the cowboy was quite standard across the west.

The nature of these drives to the Kootenays was determined by the narrow mountain trails that had to be travelled. As no wagon could navigate the trails, the cook used a bell-mare to carry the rawhide boxes containing cooking utensils and food supplies, consisting of the standard flour for bannocks, bacon, beans and coffee. The cattle faithfully followed the lead of the bell-mare, never deviating from their single file format until they stopped for grazing at noon and at the end of the day.

One of Pat Burns' main suppliers during the mining boom was the Richter Ranch, which comprised close to 10,000 acres by the turn of the century and carried 1500 head of cattle. The Richters would gather their cattle from the lower winter ranges in May and move them to their summer range near Princeton in preparation for drives to the West Kootenays. Later in the fall, they would round up the remaining cattle so that the spring and summer calves could be branded and the cattle driven to the winter feeding ground near Keremeos where large amounts of hay had been cut and stacked.

Ed Richter, who was on many of these drives, told of one late fall drive of 250 head of cattle in the early 1890s, just at the start of the mining boom. From Keremeos, the cattle were trailed over the Richter Pass to Osoyoos, then over Anarchist Mountain to Rock Creek and on to Midway and Boundary Falls. From there they were driven to Grand Forks, which at that time was little more than a cluster of shacks and a store where they could stock up with supplies for the final push. From Grand Forks, they proceeded to Christina Creek and then up over the summits to P. Burns and Company's slaughterhouse at Rossland, where they left 50 head of cattle. That was the easy part. The cowboys then left the Dewdney Trail and drove the remaining 200 head on to Castlegar. Burns and Company's main slaughterhouse at Robson was on the other side of the Columbia River; the cowboys' challenge was to swim the cattle across safely. The Richters shrewdly hired two Native men in canoes to "ride herd" on the cattle while they crossed the river. Gathering 15 to 20 head at a time, the cowboys would run them into the river, while the Native men, one at the upstream side and one on the downstream, would prod them along, driving them to the opposite shore. It took 10 trips to cross the entire herd, but they did not lose a single head. The entire trip from Keremeos to Robson took 20 days, a long and difficult drive over rough terrain.

Law and Order

The early British Columbia ranching frontier can be characterized as generally orderly and law abiding. The population was relatively small and the need for mutual support meant that people generally got along well together. However, there were occasional exceptions to the rule. Personalities would eventually clash and disagreements between neighbours would cause tension and harsh words. Most often, differences of opinion were nothing more than that and were soon resolved. But sometimes real animosities developed and matters could only be resolved in court.

When the Crown Colony of British Columbia was established in 1858, the British legal system was part of the package. Included in this system was the concept of appointing Justices of the Peace (JPs), who were responsible for the administration of civil law in a given district. These unpaid JPs were most often local landowners who were regarded as wise, although usually not particularly familiar with legal issues. For more serious cases, a magistrate's court, consisting of three JPs, could be assembled.

While serious crime was far from common on the frontier, the darker side of the human personality was occasionally revealed in crimes ranging from drunkenness and vandalism to murder and rape. Constables who were located in most towns and cities would arrest suspected criminals and hold them until they could be tried. Criminal cases were handled by judges who travelled a regular circuit and held criminal trials or "assizes" in the district where the accused was being held in jail. This system was based on the notion that persons accused of crimes should be tried by their peers in the locality where the crime was committed.

There were two areas where the court system in early British Columbia was significantly different from that of today. First, and most significantly, the legal system in the province reflected a drastically different attitude towards race. There is no question that Native people and Chinese were treated quite differently from their White neighbours. These two visible minorities were judged more harshly and punished more severely than Whites. Special laws were enacted, such as the ones that prevented Natives or Chinese persons from pre-empting land and the series of discriminatory acts directed against Chinese immigration into British Columbia. In these instances, the legal system simply reflected the attitudes and prejudices of society in general at the time.

Unlike modern courts, the legal system in the early days of settlement also tended to judge property offences more harshly than violent crimes. For example, a conviction for stealing a saw brought a sentence of 6 months in prison; stealing 16 bags of wheat brought a sentence of 18 months; and conviction for cattle rustling resulted in a 5-year jail term. It is probably not surprising that a heavier emphasis was placed on punishing property crimes on the frontier where the difference between survival and disaster was often very small. The practical value of a saw or a bag of wheat often far outweighed its monetary value to a struggling settler.

Alfred Goodwin

One interesting legal case was between Alfred Goodwin and the Douglas Lake Ranch. Goodwin and his brother, Fred, had pre-empted land near Fish Lake, northeast of the Douglas Lake Ranch, in 1891. Late that same year, the brothers acquired an additional three half-sections when the 29-square mile Marsh Meadows opened up for acquisition. This land bordered the Douglas Lake Ranch on the west and needed a fence to separate the two herds of cattle. Douglas Lake manager J.B. Greaves and Alfred Goodwin agreed to share the cost of constructing a rail fence to separate their properties and contracted James Madden, the Big Kid, to do the work. J.B. Greaves freely left the terms of the contract up to Goodwin but was prepared to cover half the costs.

Some time after the fence construction had begun, Greaves was talking to the Big Kid and learned that he was being paid a good deal less than Goodwin had told Greaves. This meant that Goodwin was overcharging Greaves and keeping the extra money for himself. Greaves, never known for his calm demeanour, was infuriated. He confronted Goodwin and declared that he would construct his own fence. Two parallel fences appeared, a few feet apart and spread over miles of rangeland, mute evidence of a growing mistrust between Goodwin and Greaves.

Things did not stop there. Over the next few years, a number of incidents fuelled the animosity between the two. In 1904, Goodwin, in an attempt to increase his holdings, built a fence around a field that was Crown land. The fence was regularly broken down, especially when Douglas Lake cowboys were in the area. This did not help an already strained relationship, and in 1907 matters came to a dramatic head. Neighbouring rancher Billy Lauder was riding across Goodwin's land to purchase some cattle and noticed 25 head of horses, mostly Clydesdales, many with the distinctive lll (one eleven) brand on their shoulder blotched out. After a heated discussion with Goodwin over the age of some of the cattle he was purchasing, Lauder informed Greaves of what he had seen. Greaves sent long-time Douglas Lake cowboys Joe Coutlee and Jack Whiteford over to have a look, and they found 23 horses, 13 of which had their brands disfigured. They drove the horses to the home ranch, and Greaves sent to Nicola for Constable Walter Clark. Clark conducted a search and found two more horses. Although it was obvious what had happened, there was no concrete proof that Goodwin had taken the horses or altered their brands, so a reward of $1,500 was offered to anyone who could help in the arrest and conviction of the horse thief. The provincial government offered a further $500.

Later that year, Oliver Walker, who had been in charge of Goodwin's cattle in 1907, had a conversation with Jack Whiteford in which he confirmed that he had helped Goodwin steal the Douglas Lake horses and change their brands. Charges were then laid against Goodwin for stealing 14 two-year-old horses from the Douglas Lake Ranch and altering their brands. Further investigation saw a number of other charges laid against Alfred Goodwin.

The preliminary hearing in Kamloops uncovered much about Goodwin's dealings. Oliver Walker's evidence was the most damaging. He testified that he and Goodwin had rounded up 25 Douglas Lake horses and put 14 of them into their corrals, where they treated the brands with Fleming's Lump Jaw Cure or Spavin Cure. These salves caused a blister on the hide that would slough off, taking the lump or spavin with it. They had the same effect on brands, removing them from the hide and leaving behind a sore that would heal over, leaving only scar tissue. According to Walker, Goodwin wanted to sell the Douglas Lake horses once the sores had healed. Evidence from others indicated that Goodwin was far from honest in his dealings with any of his neighbours, being quite willing to help himself to their cattle to feed his haying crews or to boil and feed the meat to his many pigs.

In the spring assizes in Vernon, Goodwin's lawyer, A.D. McIntyre, cleverly questioned Walker's reliability, suggesting that he was the mastermind behind the scheme and that his testimony was more for the reward money rather than any desire to see justice done. Goodwin himself took the stand and denied any involvement in the matter. McIntyre was so effective that the jury failed to reach a verdict, and a new trial was set for Kamloops. After hearing the same evidence, the jury returned a verdict of "not guilty" and Goodwin was released. Wisely, he decided not to return to his ranch, preferring to lease it out and move to the Monte Creek area, away from his arch-enemy J.B. Greaves.

A.B. Knox

Haystacks functioned like bank accounts for the early British Columbia ranchers. Even though most winters were relatively mild, the occasional one would swoop out of the north and capture the land in its icy grip. The snow and cold would make it impossible for cattle to survive without winter feed, but ranchers could fall back on the hay that they had put away for just such an occasion. Cattle could feed and survive the winter if there was enough hay to last until better weather arrived. Hard experience had taught ranchers that they should invest time and money in putting up hay during the warm summer months as insurance against the harsh winters.

Tom Ellis, who ranched at the foot of Okanagan Lake, was no exception. In fact, it is safe to say that Ellis was one of the most fastidious of haymakers. One of his neighbours, Susan Allison, who, with her husband, John, had seen their herd devastated during the winter of 1879–80, wrote that "everyone on the lake lost two-thirds of their cattle that winter except Tom Ellis, who lost none."[3] This is testimony to Ellis's foresight and industry in putting up large amounts of hay.

In the unwritten code of the ranching community, it was considered one of the worst crimes of all to mess with another man's haystack, not unlike dipping into his bank account. So it was with interest and concern that Okanagan residents watched the events of 1891 when not one, not two, but three of Tom Ellis's haystacks were set on fire.

Joseph Christien, one of the original ranchers at Okanagan Mission (later Kelowna), was in financial difficulties, and in 1890 Tom Ellis, by then

a wealthy rancher, purchased Christien's ranch for the then unheard-of sum of $9,000. No doubt Ellis recognized the potential for growing hay and wintering cattle on this fertile bottomland. He hired Robert Munson to take charge of the new ranch and Munson put up three large stacks of timothy hay that fall. In December, Ellis brought a herd of cattle up the Chute Lake trail, and the next month he brought a second herd.

On the morning of January 6, 1891, Munson awoke to find that the three haystacks were on fire. He woke Ellis, but nothing could be done to save the haystacks. Ellis was furious and determined to find out who had set the fires. A powerful rancher and a man to be reckoned with, Ellis posted a reward of $250, a lot of money in those days, for information leading to

the conviction of the arsonist. It was not long before someone claimed the reward, and in February neighbouring rancher Arthur Booth Knox appeared before Alfred Postill, JP, charged with burning the haystacks.

Arthur Booth Knox came to British Columbia in 1874 and, after farming 320 acres north of Vernon, bought the former Jules Blondeaux homestead in 1883 and started growing wheat and hay. By the 1890s Knox owned 4,000 acres of bottomland and had a second ranch in Dry Valley, near present-day Winfield. Less well known than Tom Ellis, he was nonetheless a successful rancher and popular with his neighbours. In fact, he had been driving back from visiting his neighbour, Alfonse LeFevre, the evening that the fires were started.

Henry Bloom, a cowboy working for Knox at the time of the fire, gave the most damning evidence against Knox. Bloom maintained that Knox had offered him a horse and saddle and some money to

A haying crew in the South Okanagan adds the last load of hay to the haystack, which has been built to utilize two ponderosa pines for support. Haystacks were like bank accounts for the early ranchers.

set the stacks on fire. Other witnesses swore that Bloom had boasted that he would "put up a job on Knox" and the government agent, Walter Dewdney, spoke unfavourably of Bloom's character and testified that Knox was "a hard-working, industrious man." Even the plaintiff, Tom Ellis, admitted he "would not believe Bloom on oath, if it were a hindrance to him." Despite all the evidence suggesting that Bloom was only testifying for the reward money, Knox was convicted and sentenced to three years' hard labour. Arthur Booth Knox was sent to prison for a crime he denied committing, and, indeed, most residents of the Mission Valley believed he was innocent. It appeared that Tom Ellis had wanted a conviction and was given one.

But the story did not end there. The following year, Tom Ellis brought suit to recover the damages from Knox for the value of the hay. Ellis maintained that the hay, which consisted of 200 tons of first-class timothy, was worth $4,000 and he also claimed for the loss of weight to his cattle. The case was heard at the spring assizes in Kamloops. In the course of the trial, it came out that Knox had actually been in Enderby during the time Booth alleged he was offering him money to burn the hay. The jury retired and, in an hour, returned to find in favour of the defendant, A.B. Knox. Ellis was forced to cover his costs of the suit and received no recompense for his hay.

Incredibly, Knox had to complete his term! It was February of 1894 before the *Vernon News* announced that "A.B. Knox, who has been absent for some time, returned home to be warmly welcomed by his many friends, and has taken charge of his large ranch, bordering on the east boundary of Kelowna."[4] Knox continued ranching until 1904, when he sold his land to the Okanagan Fruit and Land Company, which subdivided it into town lots. Knox Mountain within Kelowna City limits is named after him.

In a final ironic twist of fate, when Knox sold his land, he sold his cattle to Tom Ellis.

Mud Pups

By the 1870s, the British Commonwealth had reached its zenith. Contemporary maps sported large splashes of red, lending truth to the maxim that "the sun never set on the British Empire." Great Britain's economy flourished as its empire grew, and a large merchant class developed out of the wave of expanding trade and commerce. John Ruskin cried out to this merchant class in 1870 when he said: "There is a destiny now possible to us, the highest ever set before a nation to be accepted or refused ... This is what England must either do or perish; she must found colonies as fast and as far as she is able, formed of her most energetic and worthiest men; seizing every piece of fruitful waste ground she can set her foot on."[5]

Ruskin's call to young men to go to the colonies and spread the obviously superior culture of England did not go unheeded. For many middle-class families whose sons and daughters had received the best education Britain could offer, it was only appropriate that they immigrate to the colonies and establish "the light of civilization" there. The colonies offered a solution for parents who were looking for a suitable place for their energetic and, at times, unbridled younger sons. Not only would the boys' energies be put to good use in furthering the cause of Empire, but there was every possibility that they could make a decent life there.

This heady call for England's "most energetic and worthiest men" did contain some intelligent and pragmatic forethought. Anxious parents recognized that their sons needed the maximum possible advantage in their new country, and that this could be best assured by placing them under the care of someone already familiar with the customs and circumstances of the land. Many parents would contact someone of good reputation who was already established in the colony and arrange for the younger son to be placed in his care and custody until the son could make his own way. Most often this involved paying the mentor for his time and trouble. The families considered cattle ranching to be an honourable profession, and the ranches of British Columbia seemed perfect for the younger sons. And so, from the 1870s on, there was an influx of well-educated and energetic young men who came at their parents' expense and stayed to make a life for themselves.

In the interior of British Columbia these apprentice ranchers were called "mud pups," a term that initially expressed the disdain of those who had paid, and continued to pay, their own way through life. However, so many mud pups stayed on and became hard-working cowboys and successful ranchers that the term lost its negative ring and eventually indicated someone who had arrived under favourable circumstances but who worked as hard as everyone else to make a go of things.

Such was the case with Hugh Peel Lane Bayliffe. This man's ancestors included the Peels, who produced two prime ministers of Britain, and the Lane family, who were mayors of Hereford. Bayliffe came as an 18-year-old to British Columbia in 1882 and presented himself to Clement Cornwall at Ashcroft Manor. Cornwall arranged for Bayliffe to work for William Roper at Cherry Creek, west of Kamloops, to learn the ranching business. Bayliffe later reported that he worked feeding cattle every day from early December until March 9 before he earned any time off—a Sunday afternoon. During that winter, he wrote home: "We are all much too big. I am so tall, in cold weather the ends of me are so far away from the centre of warmth ... I am

Roundup time, showing a woman on sidesaddle. Women of British background considered it "unladylike" to ride a western saddle.

getting so horribly mean and miserly … I hope mother will send me some socks. I try to hide the fact that mine are worn out."[6]

The young pup learned his trade well and distinguished himself with his roping skills. He became an excellent rider and was often called upon to break a cayuse that no one else could handle. William Roper was one of the first to attempt to improve his stock, importing Hereford cattle and Clydesdale horses, and Bayliffe saw the advantages of purebred stock before most ranchers even thought about it. Before long he became Roper's cow boss and took charge of driving cattle to the CPR construction camps.

A severe drought hit the interior of British Columbia in the summer of 1886, and Bayliffe, thinking it was time to start a ranch of his own, set out to find a place with good grass and water. His travels brought him to the Chilcotin plateau, which at that time was still sparsely settled. Bayliffe took a job looking after a pack train for Tom Hance and took his time to check out the country. He spent that winter in a little cabin overlooking the Chilcotin River. In the spring he was impressed with the way the Chilcotin River overflowed its banks and naturally irrigated the land. Remembering the dry Cherry Creek summers, he pre-empted a beautiful piece of land between Alexis Creek and Redstone, and went into partnership with another Englishman, Norman Lee.

To stock his ranch he went to William Roper and made an arrangement that showed the trust that had grown between the two men. He took 100 yearling heifers with the understanding that, in five years, the partners would return the original 100 plus one half of the cattle they would produce. Some Shuswap Natives from the Kamloops area helped drive the heifers and a few purebred Hereford bulls to the new ranch. However, after crossing the Fraser River at the Gang Ranch, the Shuswaps would come no farther as they were afraid of the warlike Chilcotins. They roped and banded all the heifers and Bayliffe continued alone. True to his word, Bayliffe made good his agreement, returning over 200 cows to Roper five years later.

In 1891, Bayliffe returned to England and brought back enough funds to purchase Norman Lee's share of the ranch. He also brought back a bride, Gertrude Tyndle, a daughter of the editor of *The London Times*. Mrs. Bayliffe was a skilled sidesaddle rider and regularly helped with roundups. She also owned two racehorses and entered them in races at Becher's Prairie at Riske Creek.

The Bayliffes stayed true to their upbringing, always dressing for dinner at a table set with silver and fine china. They were also enthusiastic polo players and organized games among the local settlers. When Hugh Bayliffe died in 1934, his holdings, the 3000-acre Chilanko Ranch, were taken over by his son, Gay. The Chilanko Ranch is operated by the Bayliffe family to this day.

Another mud pup who came to learn the ranching business and stayed was Robert Cecil Cotton, who came from Hampton Court, England, to the M.G. Drummond Ranch in 1897. After a year and a summer with no pay, he began to earn the grand sum of $25 a month during the winter of 1898. After learning the trade, Cotton returned to England where he obtained enough money to buy the ranch from Drummond and rename it the Cotton Ranch. He operated it until his death in 1954.

Of course, some mud pups made the most of being far from the discipline of home and took full advantage of the regular payments from "daddy" to indulge in a life of leisure. Edward Robinson was sent by his father, George Robinson of St. John's, Newfoundland, to Thomas Wood, who was a rancher in the Okanagan Valley. Wood's account book offers an insight into a less than satisfactory arrangement:

Nov. 1882—Robinson came to be trained at farming.

Dec. 18/85—His father wrote that he would pay for instruction and keep, also for damages done by his son, also he would send the money at the end of the year at the same rate as he had been paying for him in the North West $1000 a year.

Mar. 5, 1886—Sent three years pay, at the same time requested me, as his son was to begin on a ranch of his own, to stock it up for him, that was after he simply wrote requesting his money due. I stocked the ranch up to amount of $3000; the next winter all his stock died, the next spring I counted out to him a like number; he counted them after me, also him and his man took them away to his ranch.

Oct. 1886—I went to see his father who told me that the money he had sent was for me, also understanding that his son rode and kept his horses in my stock stable, that he would pay that too.

As to Robinson claiming wages for seven years all the time he was with me shooting and visiting, except 5 weeks one fall in haying time, for that he was paid in cash $50.00 at the time, like the rest of the hired men.

It is interesting to note that when Robinson arrived at Wood's ranch in 1882 he was only 17 years old. Wood was paid the handsome sum of $1,000 a year for Robinson to "be trained at farming." As the account book notes, five weeks' wages amounted to $50, so the amount paid to Wood was significant.

Klondike Cattle Drives

In the fall of 1896, a ragged group of miners got off the boat in Seattle with a fortune in their pockets. The hundreds of pounds of gold that they carried sparked a gold rush that would capture the imagination of the world and earn almost legendary status in the history books. During the next few years, tens of thousands of men and women flocked to a hitherto uncharted area known as the Klondike. By 1897 it was becoming obvious that a gold rush unlike any other was shaping up in the Yukon. Cattlemen in British Columbia, Alberta, Oregon and Washington, conscious that thousands of men and women converging on a remote area in search of gold means a demand for food, began to look for the most effective way to get cattle into the Yukon.

Miners travelling to the gold fields had the choice of four different routes—all difficult and treacherous. For the majority of gold seekers looking at a map, the most obvious route was by water to Skagway on the Alaska panhandle and then the 500- or 600-mile land and water route to Dawson in the heart of the gold fields. Most gold seekers on this route travelled inland over the White Pass to Lake Bennett, then by scow or boat through a series of lakes and rivers to the Yukon River. They could also travel from Skagway over the Chilkoot Pass to Lake Bennett or take the long overland Dalton Trail to the Yukon River.

Klondike Cattle Trails

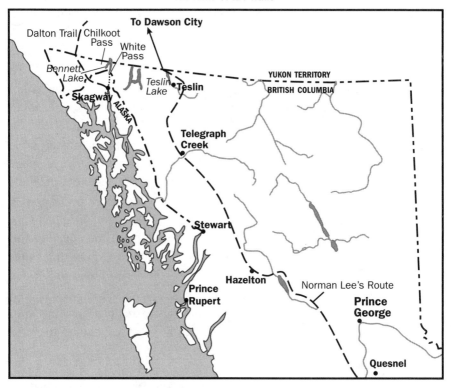

A second route followed the Yukon River from its mouth on the Bering Sea and looped up through the Arctic Circle to eventually make its way to Dawson. Even on a map this route looked difficult and dangerous and only a very few particularly hardy individuals attempted it. Then there was the overland route from Edmonton. All those who tried it rated it an utter failure because of the difficulty of the terrain and the lack of supply centres along the way. Another "all-Canadian" route started in the Chilcotin and proceeded up Alexis Creek and along the Nazko River to meet the trail constructed in the 1860s by the Collins Overland Telegraph Company. This trail had been cut as far north as Telegraph Creek but word of the successful laying of a cable across the Atlantic had brought the project to an end.

The cattlemen who saw the Klondike market as the pot of gold at the end of the rainbow faced the same alternatives. Most saw the route from Skagway as the most promising, and the first to attempt it was William Thorpe of Seattle, who brought in 25 head of cattle over the White Pass in the fall of 1897. He slaughtered the cattle as soon as he arrived and sold them at an immense profit. Another cattleman who cast a hungry eye at the Klondike market was the legendary Pat Burns, who operated butcher shops in the

Kootenays and in Alberta. He arranged for Billy Perdue to purchase oxen in Seattle then drive them over the same route, arriving shortly after Thorpe and meeting with the same financial success.

Over the next three years, Burns made regular drives into the Klondike and used the cattle and the cowboys of British Columbia extensively. He bought cattle from the ranches in the Thompson/Nicola and Gang Ranch areas and engaged any cowboys that he could from these suppliers to accompany the cattle by rail to Vancouver and by scow to Skagway. The usual procedure was to load the cattle and about 20 horses on a 1,200-ton CPR scow that was pulled at the end of a long cable by a tug boat. There were pens on the scow for the cattle and a small cabin for the cowboys. The cattle were unloaded at Pyramid Harbour, across the inlet from Skagway. From Skagway, the cowboys started out on the difficult overland Dalton Trail, originally cut by Jack Dalton. Needless to say, Dalton and his well-armed men were at the start of the trail to collect a "toll" for the right to use the trail. Grazing along the trail was generally poor, and cattle had to eat willow leaves and twigs as they travelled. The scarcity of feed along the trail became worse as the summer of 1898 progressed, and as the undiscriminating cattle ate anything green, there was a real danger of them succumbing to toxic plants. To make matters worse, the rocky trail ground the cattle's feet to the quick, making them lame and unable to walk any further. Nonetheless, the years of 1898, 1899 and 1900 saw thousands of head of cattle reach Dawson City and sell for as high as a dollar a pound. Every bit of the cow was utilized. The meat was readily sold; the bones went for soup; and the offal and hides were boiled up with oat or corn meal for dog food.

Joe Payne, who had been the cow boss for the Douglas Lake Ranch for over a decade, was one of the first to sign up with Pat Burns and take cattle to the Klondike. Ulus Campbell, son of Kamloops area rancher Lewis Campbell, and Izzy Knapp, another Kamloops area cowboy, also drove cattle into the Yukon. Joe Payne stayed on and worked for Pat Burns for many years afterward.

But the pioneering cattlemen of the Chilcotin looked at the "all-B.C." route and figured that they could make it to the gold fields that way. The spring of 1898 saw a flurry of activity as a number of Chilcotin ranchers began to assemble herds for the trail north. In fact, when the snows finally disappeared from the shady trails and valleys, there was a scramble to see who would be first on the trail. It was rightly assumed that those who were first to arrive would enjoy the best opportunity to sell their cattle.

The distinction of being the first enterprising cattleman to head his cattle north from the Chilcotin to the Klondike gold fields went to Jim Cornell, a native of Tennessee who had established a ranch on Fraser Flats above the

Chilcotin River near Riske Creek. He headed north with about 100 head of cattle in early May of 1898. He was joined by Varish "French" Henri, who was born in Ontario and had worked for Billy Pinchbeck, Billy Adams and Bill Robinson. Henri bought 25 head of cattle with his savings and threw in with Cornell on the long trip north.

Cornell and Henri were closely followed by Jerry Gravelle with 100 head of cattle, Norman Lee with 200 head and Johnny Harris with another 200 head. Predictably, there was a keen sense of competition between those in charge of the various drives. Not only was there a push to be first to the good overnighting areas, but the first herds over the trail rapidly depleted the grazing along the way, leaving little for the ones following behind. This lack of good forage was further complicated by the mud that the hundreds of gold seekers with horses and mules who were also on the trail churned up along the way.

Fortunately for us, the diary kept by Norman Lee on his epic cattle drive north, which chronicles the day-to-day routines and hardships on the trail, survived its remarkable journey and has given us a unique insight into the experience.[7] Lee left his Chilcotin ranch on May 17 with five cowboys, mostly Chilcotin Natives, a "boss packer" with nine pack horses, and a cook. The herd was usually split up with each cowboy driving a band of about 30 or 40 head. This made it easier to keep track of the cattle in the thick bush and allowed the herd to split up and graze on whatever they could find. While the cattle were fresh, they made about 10 to 12 miles a day, but fallen timber along the way made the going tough. At the beginning, since the cattle were still close to home, night herding was necessary and Lee noted cynically in his diary that night herding "in a pouring rain is the reverse of pleasant."

The usual daily routine was to get up early and start the cattle before the sun was too strong, leaving the cook to pack up camp and push the pack train forward. Spare saddle horses were driven on ahead of the cattle, with the wrangler being responsible

Norman Lee lost everything attempting to drive cattle to the Klondike.

Native Chilcotin cowboys at the Cotton Ranch, near Riske Creek. When colder weather came, cowboy fashion sometimes took a back seat to warmth.

for finding a good feeding ground for the noon stop. The pack train and cook would pass the drive during the day and push on to locate a good spot to overnight. As the trail provided few good places for camping, sometimes the cook and pack train would go too far for a normal day's travel by the herd, leaving Lee and the others to do their best for a camp spot.

Several weeks into the drive, Johnny Harris and his herd overtook Lee's herd, leaving Lee as the last of the four herds heading north. Grazing from Fraser Lake to Hazelton was good, so at this stage being the last in line did not pose a problem, but later on, when grazing was scanty, it created real problems as the cattle set about eating anything green they could find. One steer in Lee's herd died from eating wild larkspur, and Johnny Harris lost more than a dozen head to the same plant. Lee reported that he was advised "to bleed them by chopping off a piece of their tails and feed them much bacon grease." While the effectiveness of this remedy is questionable, Lee certainly did not lose any more cattle to poisonous plants.

During the drive to Hazelton, one of Lee's Native cowboys became homesick, and his cook became just plain sick. Both of them turned back and headed home, leaving Lee to try to convince two of the gold seekers on the trail to take the slower mode of travel and work for him along the way. Another Native cowboy left at Hazelton, and the rest of the cowboys were able to buy some HBC rum, extending the expected layover in Hazelton from three to six days. Luckily for Lee he managed to sell a few head to the Hudson's Bay officer to pay for supplies.

From Hazelton to Telegraph Creek, shortage of feed was becoming a serious problem. The trail wound its way through heavy timber and mud flats, with only an occasional swamp with grass to feed the cattle. On top of that, the trail was a sea of mud, a result of the hundreds of animals that had passed on ahead of them combined with a wet summer. The muddy trail and the frequent river crossings began to take their toll on the hooves of the cattle and horses, particularly the horses. They became victims of what the cowboys termed "mud fever," which left the horses lame and useless for riding. As more of the horses became lame and had to be shot, Lee was forced to have his men walk with the cattle, leaving the healthy horses to carry their food and camp supplies. Eventually all of the horses were gone, and the men slogged on, weary and footsore.

On August 25 they were at the summit of the mountain range, 260 miles from Hazelton, travelling close to the snow line and crossing innumerable glacier streams, swift and cold. Lee walked on ahead and made his way to Telegraph Creek, purchasing flour and bacon for his crew and caching it in the woods, "blazing a tree with my cow brand, so the boys would know where to find the stuff." He arrived at Telegraph Creek on September 2, ahead of his cattle, and found that Jim Cornell and "French" Henri, who had made better time with their smaller herd, had decided not to go any farther. They had spotted an opportunity to take advantage of the steady flow of hungry men along this trail to the gold fields and had no need to continue on their arduous journey. Cornell took over a butcher shop previously owned by Dominic Burns, brother of the famous Pat Burns, and sold his fresh beef for 75 cents a pound. Both Cornell and Henri were making a tidy profit on their cattle but the demand was not great enough for Lee to call a halt to his cattle drive.

Lee's only hope was to press on to Teslin, where the cattle could be slaughtered and the dressed beef rafted over lake and river to Dawson. He returned to his cattle and sent a man ahead to build scows at Teslin. Finally, on October 3, Lee and his weary cowboys arrived at Teslin. There they found Johnny Harris in the process of butchering his cattle and building scows to carry them to Dawson. Jerry Gravelle, broke and disillusioned, had arranged to have his beef shipped with Harris's. Within a few days, Harris was off on his scows and Lee, using Harris's corrals, started slaughtering in earnest. He hired an experienced butcher who could dress 20 head of cattle per day while his crew managed another 20. The slaughtering was completed at the same time as the two scows, each measuring 16 by 40 feet. Although the beef was not good, it would still sell for a dollar a pound in Dawson.

The scows set off on October 17, with a good breeze blowing them along. After two days of good sailing, the wind began to pick up and the lake became extremely rough. By now the scows were threatening to break apart, so the men began to look for a sheltered cove along the lakeshore. Finding no shelter, in desperation they ran their scows onto the rocky shore. The gale continued to blow for two more days, and the continuous beating of the scows on the rocks wrecked one and then the other, leaving the beef lying in the shallow water. There was nothing that could be done. It was too late to construct other scows, and there was no one around who was interested in buying the beef. Lee had little choice but to accept defeat and abandon the beef. The men divided up the food supplies, and most of them decided to salvage enough lumber from the scows to construct boats and proceed on to Dawson. Only one man, Will Copeland, decided to return south with Norman Lee.

The fate of Johnny Harris, who had preceded Lee by four days, was not much better. Although he had escaped the fateful storm on the lake, his scows had become frozen in about 200 miles above Dawson, and his beef, like Lee's, was a complete loss.

Lee and Copeland constructed a hand sleigh on which to carry their few belongings and began the long trip home. They hoped to get down the Stikine River before it froze over, but the heavy snows made travel extremely difficult, and they abandoned the sled. Finding the Stikine frozen over, they tramped over ice and snow for 100 miles to the Alaska boundary, arriving there on Christmas Day. After more delays, they got across to Wrangel and took passage south. Norman Lee arrived in Vancouver "with a roll of blankets, a dog and one dollar—the latter I took the first opportunity of exchanging for some refreshments, and made a fresh start with a clean sheet." After borrowing enough money to take the train to Ashcroft and borrowing a horse to ride home, Norman Lee started ranching again. By 1902, he was well on the way to prosperity again, and his descendents continue to ranch in the Chilcotin to this day.

The Cowboy Without His Horse

Cowboys are generally happiest when they are sitting in the saddle on a tall horse and working cattle. In fact, it might even be said that the cowboy, when off his horse, is not a cowboy at all. However, on the smaller ranches of the early days in particular, the cowboy was often called upon to perform a number of tasks that he might consider demeaning. Luckily, the cowboy is a loyal creature and, albeit begrudgingly at times, accepted the less romantic jobs like riding a hay mower instead of a horse or taking on the dreaded chore of fencing with barbed wire.

When the influx of more and more settlers to the B.C. interior marked the end of the open range, barbed wire fences sprang up to enclose the once open ranges. Fencing therefore occupied much of the cowboy's time between summer turn-out and fall roundup. No job was more greatly despised than that of struggling to pull taut a wire loaded with sharp barbs ready to tear into the innocent cowboy's flesh. Barbed wire came in unwieldy rolls that added to the difficulty of the job. On one ranch in the Okanagan, the rolls were delivered on the beach from a scow and then had to be manhandled to the top of a steep bank before being loaded onto wagons. The rancher refused to use a horse to drag the rolls of barbed wire up the bank, insisting that it was easier and cheaper for the men to do the job. After wrestling a few rolls up the bank, one of the cowboys said in disgust, "To hell with this," and allowed a roll of wire to bounce down the hill and into the lake, narrowly missing the rancher on the way down. The roll of wire gathered considerable momentum in its downward trek and disappeared into the depths of the lake. After that a horse was used for hauling the expensive wire up the bank.

Even though cowboys hated fencing with barbed wire, it was at least considered a "manly" activity. The same could not be said for milking. Despite being surrounded by thousands of head of cows, cowboys seldom had a supply of fresh milk. The average working cowboy would rather be caught dead than be found squatting down milking a cow. Harry Marriott, who worked for the Gang Ranch, expressed surprise that, on unloading a freight wagon he had driven to the Gang Ranch, he

> saw a box of butter labeled from New Zealand. Afterwards I found out that although the Gang Ranch had over seven thousand head of beef cattle they did not go in for butter making ... Cowboys and cattlemen have always shied away from cow milking, for some reason or another. It seemed to me that somewhere along the line it hurt their dignity somehow, as they regarded cow milking as one of the lowest down jobs that a human being could fall heir to doing.
>
> Cowboys and Indians would, and could, do 'most everything with cattle, drive them, rope them, brand and castrate them, and may other jobs necessary to the cow business, but to ask them to milk cows, "No Sir." It was taboo to them.[8]

Hugh Walkem, who wrote a series of articles for the *Ottawa Citizen* in 1881 that later appeared in the Kamloops *Inland Sentinel*, wrote about the lack of fresh milk: "The bachelors, who of course do not make butter, do not pretend to have milk either summer or winter, not because they cannot obtain milch cows, but I expect because it's too much trouble to milk, and as they become weaned, as it were, soon regard milk as a luxury rather than a necessary of life, although I don't think there is one of them who would not endorse the wish or whatever you might call it ... 'Give me the luxuries of life and I can dispense with the necessities.'"[9]

Some ranches, however, kept milk cows, and if there was no "lady of the house" to do the milking, the cowboys would begrudgingly take a turn at milking after the day's work was done. Ed Carruthers, who worked as a ranch hand for the Lequime outfit near present-day Kelowna, managed to avoid his turn because he was missing the middle two fingers on his right hand due to an accident as a boy. However, one Saturday evening he was the only man not heading into Kelowna, so the foreman told him that he would just have to do the best he could. When he thought they had all left, he settled down to do the milking which, of course, he was able to do quite well. He was disturbed from his task by the voice of the foreman yelling from behind him, "You so and so son of a gun [or words to that effect], so you can milk! Well, you'll do your share from now on."[10]

Carruthers also told the story of another domestic incident that illustrates the dearth of dairy products in the cowboy's life. He was working on a different ranch for an "old-time" rancher whose wife was considered "close" with the grub provided for the cowboys. Their regular meal was usually sowbelly, applesauce and green tea. Now the wife, like so many of the women on the isolated ranches, looked forward to the occasional visit of the travelling Protestant preacher who would offer a more sympathetic ear for her story of loneliness and privation. On one occasion, the visiting preacher was asked to give the blessing before supper, but, ever keen to give all a chance for inclusion in the work of the kingdom, he suggested that one of the cowboys say grace. Immediately, a Cockney English cowboy claimed he was up to the task and prayed as follows:

Oh Lord when hunger presses sore,
Wilt Thou stand us in Thy stead,
And from Thy bounteous store above,
Send us butter for our bread.

As all the cowboys at the table hunched over their plates to hide their grins, the rancher's wife turned several shades of red.[11]

Domestic duties were taboo to the average working cowboy. It was one thing to cook up the grub for you and your partner when sharing a cabin in a remote range for winter-feeding, and some cowboys displayed a genuine talent for transforming the dried and powdered ingredients that were packed into the high country into quite passable fare, but when they were at the home site, the extent of their domestic duties was happily limited to washing up before dinner. Food preparation could be left to the cook, who was generally an older retired cowboy who simply couldn't leave the ranching life or the wife of the rancher. But occasionally, even the most macho cowboy could not avoid kitchen duty as Charlie Simms, who was working for Thomas Wood at his Winfield Ranch in the Okanagan, found out to his cost. It was the practice of the bachelor cowboys on Winfield Ranch to spend the weekend at Okanagan Mission where the Lequimes ran an excellent stopping house and saloon. Each weekend, one cowboy had to stay behind to keep an eye on the cattle. So it fell that Charlie was asked to stay behind and, as Thomas Wood

Cowboys wait for the ferry to Kelowna, where they'll attend the Kelowna Fall Fair. The cowboys all look freshly laundered and on their way to having a good time.

departed to town, was told to have some beans boiled and ready for Monday. Charlie, ever eager to please his boss, hunted around and found some beans and put them on to boil for a couple of hours. On Sunday morning, they did not seem to be cooked enough, so Charlie put them on to boil some more … and some more. Sunday evening arrived, and the beans had not lost their flinty characteristics. When Tom Wood arrived home from town, he inquired whether Charlie had cooked the beans as requested. Charlie replied, "Well, Mr. Wood, I have been cooking some, but it seems to me they are taking an awfully long time to cook." Tom Wood had arrived in the Okanagan in 1867 and "batched" for many years, so he was reasonably experienced in the domestic arts. He remarked that sometimes beans were a little slow to get just right and perhaps a little soda would help. He lifted the lid and immediately uncovered the problem—Charlie had boiled up the winter supply of coffee beans. He was never asked to cook again.

Fun and Games

A cowboy's life was not all hard work and long hours. Quiet times on the ranch offered a much-needed opportunity to let off steam and to engage in the competitions and discussions typical of young men everywhere. Inevitably the activities centred on horses and livestock and, not surprisingly, the competitions usually involved activities on horseback.

However, some of the games that the cowboys played were a little less predictable. For those who were of British extraction and spent most of their working days in the saddle, it seemed logical to organize games of polo. The first recorded game in Kamloops was played in 1890 and was an informal fun match between eight local cowboys. There was no question about the cowboys' ability as horsemen, but striking the ball with the long-handled mallet proved to be more of a challenge—much to the amusement of the few spectators who came along for the fun. That first game ended at 0:0, but practice makes perfect, and before long the cowboys had become more adept at the finer points of the game. The Kamloops Polo Club was formed in 1897, with William Roper of Cherry Creek as the Honourary President. Roper enthusiastically

Although the men on this polo team near Kamloops are suitably attired from the head down, the cowboy hats are a tip-off.

supported the game and, in 1898, donated the Roper Cup, which he had brought in from England. Teams from all over the interior of British Columbia competed for the Roper Cup. Hugh Bayliffe organized a team of Alexis Creek and Riske Creek cowboys that regularly competed, and teams from Grande Prairie (today's Westwold) also travelled to Kamloops to compete.

Polo

Polo was especially popular in the Nicola Valley at Nicola and Quilchena. Every Sunday afternoon, a match was organized at one of the two places, followed by a visit to the Quilchena Hotel or the Druid Hotel in Nicola. The countryside introduced a few natural hazards that may not be considered standard in the "galloping game." One Sunday afternoon the hot competition at Nicola came to an abrupt halt when a skunk made its leisurely way across the playing field. On another occasion, a coyote made the mistake of crossing the field, and the polo players immediately became "fox" hunters for the rest of the afternoon.

In 1896, the Nicola team was invited to Victoria to compete in what is considered the first polo tournament ever conducted in British Columbia. The Nicola team consisted of former British Army regulars Captain H.R. Cholmondelay, Captain A.C. Bald and cowboys Broadbent and Nash, proving that true sportsmanship transcends class distinctions. The only difficulty was that the Nicola players, who had the wisdom and foresight

A polo game in progress on the open rangeland around Kamloops. The British Columbia interior was a hotbed of polo in the early 1900s.

to bring nine ponies along, had to ride and drive their horses 50 miles to the nearest railway station at Spences Bridge. They then had to travel by rail, sea and road to arrive in Victoria three days later. Obviously one of the team members must have had the money to support his enthusiasm and foot the bill for all the travel costs, but it all turned out very well when the Nicola team beat the Victoria and Cowichan teams and only narrowly lost by a single point to the Royal Navy team in the final few seconds of the game.

The Westwold team was formed in 1898 and, with the help of excellent Douglas Lake horses, won the Roper Cup every year from 1901 to 1906. In 1901, the team consisted of Walter Homfray of the Adelphi Ranch, George Harding, Frank Gordon and George Butler. A combination of these four, along with Charlie Johnson, formed the winning team in each of the six years.

Even more bizarre was the custom of the Cornwall brothers, Clement and Henry, whose lineage could be traced as far back as Richard I in the 12th century. The Cornwalls pre-empted land on the Thompson River in 1862 and established a successful ranch and stopping house, building the core of Ashcroft Manor, which still stands to this day, in 1863. As Englishmen to the core, the brothers decided that one of their country's most exhilarating sports should be imported into the Colony of British Columbia. And what could be more English than riding to hounds? In 1868, they imported four foxhounds from their native Gloucestershire. One of the four died on the long trip around the Horn, but the remaining three, Ringwood, Rapid and Daisy, formed the nucleus of the famous Cornwall hounds.

The brothers' next problem was finding foxes to chase, for foxes in the interior of British Columbia are scarce indeed. But the Cornwalls were undeterred. In the absence of foxes, they would chase coyotes, which were plentiful as well as larger and faster than foxes. With the problem of quarry resolved, the brothers had no problem persuading their neighbouring ranchers to join in the fun. Some even went to the expense of purchasing red coats to make the scene even more "a little bit of England."

The hunt would begin about 10 in the morning, and if the neighbours were otherwise occupied, the party would only include Clement and Henry accompanied by their Native cowboy, Harry. Often the hunt would last all day, and on one occasion the exuberant huntsmen did not drag themselves home until 1:00 a.m. the following morning. Often Harry, who had better hearing and eyesight than the brothers, would race ahead with the pack instead of staying behind to whip up the stragglers among the dogs. However, the Cornwalls were good sports and always spoke highly of him.

The hunts continued well into the 1880s. The November 25, 1886, Kamloops *Inland Sentinel* has an account of "Gov. Cornwall's Hounds" (Clement Cornwall was lieutenant governor of British Columbia by then) and describes a series of hunts with the Cornwall pack in the Nicola Valley. With 11 men and 5 women, hounds and horses all hosted by William Pooley, a hunt was held on Monday, Wednesday and Friday. On each occasion, a coyote was scented and a merry chase took place. Happily for the coyote, the Nicola country has abundant heavy brush and rocky areas, and in each case the coyote sought refuge in an inaccessible place. On the Monday, the entire pack disappeared into the heavy brush and was not recovered until the following day. The article observed:

> There is nothing like hunting of this sort to bring together pleasantly both friends and strangers for a day's innocent, manly and healthful recreation. Few, indeed, who have once followed the flying pack would fail to miss another opportunity of doing so. The Messrs. Cornwall, in keeping a pack of hounds at great trouble and expense for the amusement of the country in general, are worthy of far more support than they have generally met with. Mr. William Roper of Cherry Creek, has frequently entertained them at his place, and on one occasion, we believe Mr. Vernon of Cold

The Cornwall Ranch at Ashcroft. Clement and Henry Cornwall were enthusiastic supporters of the hunt in the B.C. interior.

Stream, otherwise no interest, or very little seems to have been shown. An invitation for next season from some of the principal ranchers of the neighbourhood, would be an excellent idea and would give all of us an opportunity of becoming partakers of that sport which is alike 'fit for king and peasant.'"[12]

Sadly, the hounds failed to thrive in the Ashcroft country and were often quite sick. Perhaps inbreeding or nutritional deficiency contributed to their bad health. A rancher from Manitoba bought them, and, as Clement Cornwall wrote in his diary, "the glory of Ashcroft departed." He followed this entry with a verse:

> I have lived my life, I am nearly done,
> But I freely admit that the best of my fun
> I had to horse and hound.

Horse Races

Give a man a horse and he will ride it. Give two men each a horse and they will want to know which one is fastest. Horse racing began in British Columbia almost as soon as the first horses arrived.

Keremeos, for example, hosted a regular Sunday gathering at the local store. Races were usually held at a bench below the town, but the big race meetings took place on a long bench above the river on Manuel Barcelo's ranch. In 1872 this was the site of the famous race between Barrington Price's Mountain Chief and Jim McConnell's Bulgar Dick. A large gathering of Natives and Whites assembled for the race, giving a festive air to the occasion. J.C Haynes, former government agent at Osooyos, was the judge, and he stepped off the mile distance. Natives and Whites circulated around, chatting, shaking hands and making wagers on the outcome of the race. As there was very little currency circulating in the early days, wagers were most often made with personal belongings, everything from horse tack to blankets and clothing. Excitement and cheering, along with dejection among the losers, greeted the winner, Mountain Chief, as it crossed the finish line. The race was one of the earliest recorded in the Okanagan Valley and was the topic of conversation and debate for many years to come.

Up in the Cariboo, Benjamin Franklin "Doc" English, an avid horseracing enthusiast, indulged in his true passion, the thrill of the race. In 1873 he had taken up 320 acres of benchland on the west side of the Fraser River that had been known as Deer Park since gold-rush days and used that land to pursue his first love. One horse that he brought back from San Francisco was called "Nigger Baby" (at a time when that epithet was not considered racist), a speedy black horse. Wherever there is one fast horse, another is not far behind, and soon a fellow racing enthusiast from Williams Lake challenged Doc to pit his horse against the best Williams Lake had to offer, a sorrel whose name was not recorded. Nigger Baby won going away, but the owner of the sorrel, not to be deterred, offered to race again, and in a tradition as old as horse racing itself, large amounts of money were wagered. The two owners, again in keeping with tradition, decided quietly between themselves that the sorrel would win this time.

Doc English, in a magnanimous gesture, let his friend Phil Grinder, who had first settled at Alkali Lake with Otto Bowe back in the 1860s, in on the scheme. But Doc expressed his concern that Nigger Baby might prove difficult to hold back in the excitement of the race, and so he proposed that he and Grinder administer an arsenic pill to the horse to ensure the outcome. Grinder agreed to prepare the pill and administer it before the race. In the meantime, he bet every penny he could get his hands on that the sorrel would win ... and there were many takers. Just before the race, Grinder appeared at the stable with an arsenic pill wrapped in a lump of bread to make it easier to administer. As he struggled to open the horse's powerful jaws, Doc offered to hold the bread. Grinder had no reason to

mistrust his fellow conspirator and, once he had the horse's mouth open, inserted the lump of dough Doc handed him. But oh the fickleness of human nature! Doc had switched more than just the lump of dough on Grinder. He had watched the betting and long before decided that more money could be won by backing Nigger Baby. Needless to say, Nigger Baby won going away, with Phil Grinder left watching in slack-jawed dismay. There was nothing he could say or do, having made his own bed. But one can be sure Doc English never appeared on Grinder's list of "friends" again.

Early horse-race scene in the Okanagan Valley. Everyone in the community came out for horse races, which were usually followed by a dance or social.

Tom Stevenson, who cowboyed for the Postill Ranch in the Okanagan in the 1880s, tells the story of a famous race that took place near Priest's Valley (now Vernon) on Victoria Day, May 24, 1887. The race was between Alf Postill's Roney and Louis Bercier's Mountain Chief (obviously not the same horse of that name owned by Barrington Price some 15 years earlier). Mountain Chief and all the old-time ranchers turned up chatting and exchanging news. Excitement ran high and the betting even higher as race time approached. Stevenson, who had helped to train Roney, found that before he knew it, he had bet most of his winter wages on his favourite. As he headed away from the noisy bunch of bettors, he met an Okanagan Native cowboy with a little Appalousa stock horse that he was willing to bet on Mountain Chief. Stevenson tried to wager his own saddle horse for the Appalousa, but instead the Native man eyed his new double-rigged Cheyenne saddle and offered to bet his horse for the saddle. Off came the saddle, straight onto the Appalousa, winner take all.

Cornelius O'Keefe, who owned most of the land on either side of the race area, paced off a mile-long stretch along the Okanagan Landing road. E.J. Tronson, Okanagan Chief Paul and Price Ellison acted as judges. Finally the horses were off, head and head. At the quarter, Mountain Chief led by four lengths with Bercier laying on the quirt. Postill rode low and easy, not laying a hand on Roney. At the half, Bercier looked to be pulling away as he was six lengths ahead, still laying on the whip. By the three-quarter mark, his lead was reduced to three lengths, and Postill was riding hard and gaining. In the stretch, with Bercier still a length in front, spectators began to close in from behind, shooting their six-guns in the air. Now both riders were laying on the quirt as they crossed the finish line with Roney in the lead by half a length. Stevenson swung up on his new Appalousa horse and rode off.

More races followed as the afternoon passed away, and in the evening the furniture was moved out of the dining room in Tronson's Hotel to allow for dancing until daybreak. The few Native and white women present were in high demand as each cowboy was determined to dance as often as possible. As the grey dawn was breaking, a tired but happy throng of cowboys mounted up and headed off to their respective ranches for a hard day's work. Happiest of all was Stevenson as he rode tall in the saddle of his new stock horse.

The Chilcotin Native people held regular weekly races near Ed and Helen Sherringham's ranch at Chezacut, and once a year the entire district converged on Becher's Prairie for a race meet. The prairie was named after Fred Becher, who ran a saloon, trading post and stopping house at Riske Creek. Becher became the postmaster of the Chilcoten (as it was spelled in those days) Post Office in 1894 and the yearly festivities took place around his place. Races lasted for up to an entire week, giving everyone from Riske Creek to Redstone, Native people and Whites alike, a chance to get together with their neighbours. Everyone would camp out on the prairie, betting on their favourite horses during the daytime and visiting into the night. One year, Doc English brought in two horses from San Francisco and convinced his old partner, Tom Hance, to bet on this "sure thing." Between the two men, all bets were covered, but, to their dismay, the local horses proved to be too much for these "imports" and the two lost their shirts. Undeterred,

Doc English returned the next year, determined to make good his losses. He suspected that his jockey had been "bought" so he substituted 12-year-old Jimmy Isnardy instead. Jimmy was so light that his opponents insisted he fasten weights to his saddle to even things out. While the horses were lining up to start, Doc went out to calm his excitable horse (and returned with the weights stowed carefully in his pocket). His horse won and Doc was a happy man again.

By 1900 a formal racetrack was laid out at Becher's Prairie on the site of many an earlier race. The week-long gathering also featured dancing at Becher's big house nearby. The annual Becher's Ball became an institution in the Chilcotin with people coming from as far away as Williams Lake and Soda Creek. The Bechers remained in the area until 1941.

Chapter Five

THE CHANGING FACE OF RANCHING

The Big Ranches

Harry Marriott was born in England and came to British Columbia in 1907. After working at odd jobs in British Columbia and Washington State for five years, he took the train north to Ashcroft, intending to find work on a ranch in the Cariboo Chilcotin. In Ashcroft he ran into Andrew Stobie, who offered him a job at the Gang Ranch. Nine days later, on June 7, 1912, Marriott got his first glimpse of the famous ranch:

> At the top of a bunch-grass slope the road turned down the sloping hill. What a panorama of size and beauty met my gaze! I saw green hay fields, at least six hundred acres of them, and a cluster of buildings sitting in amidst some native poplar and tall straight Lombardy poplar trees.
>
> This was the Gang Ranch, the finest sight any ranch man would ever like to see.[1]

Marriott went on to describe some of the buildings in the ranch headquarters, including "a small lumber house which was the store. In it were supplies of all kinds, from Hudson Bay blankets to plain chewing tobacco." There was also "a large-sized house that was covered with a light tin sheeting and painted red," which was the bunkhouse. The Gang Ranch had been bought by a syndicate, the Western Canadian Ranching Company, from Thaddeus Harper in 1888 and was an immense operation, covering some 60,000 acres of deeded land plus pastoral land leased from the province.

By the turn of the century, ranching in the B.C. interior had gone from being a family occupation to becoming big business. Large companies owned many ranches and used them as investments, installing management staff

Thorlakson boys roping a horse on the Commonage near Vernon. The first cowboy will not hold his rope for long unless the second one gets his loop on the horse.

Prior to the construction of the Gang Ranch Bridge in 1911, all supplies had to be ferried across the river and horses or cattle swum across.

and carefully monitoring profit and loss. Most of these companies also had their own butcher shops. In many ways, this had the effect of stabilizing the ranching industry by providing continuity through the cycles of good and bad winters and price fluctuations, and by providing an outlet for smaller ranches to sell their cattle. This was especially true of the Douglas Lake Cattle Company whose manager, J.B. Greaves, would buy cattle from the ranchers of the Okanagan and Nicola, paying them in the fall and picking up his cattle in the spring, and thus providing the ranchers with much-needed cash during the difficult winter months.

One change in the industry that arose from the move to large cattle ranches was the development of the more specialized role of the cowboy. Smaller ranches needed their hands to do everything from haying to fencing as well as handling cattle, but the larger ranches had the luxury of hiring

workers for specific tasks and keeping a large group of men who spent all day every day on horseback handling cattle. In the B.C. interior, these cowboys, or cowpunchers, were called "riders" because riding is pretty much all they did.

The Gang Ranch was managed for many years by J.D. Prentice with Andrew Stobie, who had been Prentice's "gillie" (attendant) in Scotland, in charge of operations. Jim Steward was the cow boss, or head cowboy in charge of cattle.

Alexander Gillespie recalled working as a rider for the Gang Ranch in the summer of 1902. He, however, had a distinct advantage—his uncle was J.D. Prentice. "He had been manager of the Gang Ranch for some time when I went up, so things were made very easy for me and I did not have to ride any bad broncos, and the head cowboy was good to me. Life was great. I can still remember the excitement of the early morning starts, with pack horses and grub wagons, as we would go back on the Summer Range for branding roundup and long days in the saddle, punching along a bunch of cattle with calves."[2]

Ranching life must have suited Gillespie because he returned the following year to work at the Gang Ranch, spending most of his summer catching wild horses, driving them to Ashcroft and staying with them to deliver them to a buyer in Alberta.

The Coldstream Ranch near Vernon controlled about 13,000 acres but, under the ownership of Lord Aberdeen, then Governor General of Canada, had diversified and become heavily involved in growing apples as well as raising hogs and sheep alongside the traditional cattle. In the early 1900s the Coldstream employed about 100 hands in its various activities. As B. Eyre-Walker, who worked for the Ranch in 1909, recounted:

A ranch hand was not hired for his manners but for his capacity to fill some particular niche in the daily operations. The Canadians, Americans, Englishmen, Scotsmen, Irishmen, Welshmen, French Canadians, Red Indians, "Siwashes" (Half-breeds), and the various other specimens, hybrid and otherwise … all had the necessary qualifications for the jobs they held …

Ear-marking and castrating a calf. Notches or slits cut in the calf's ear were easier to spot in a herd of cattle than a brand.

Noon at the Coldstream Ranch near Vernon. The ranch was purchased by Lord Aberdeen, Governor General of Canada, in 1891.

There were nine beds in my bunk-house, an upper room in a two-storey building with one window and—being early summer—as hot as the proverbial place. All the beds were occupied in spite of the persistent attentions of bed bugs. That room had for long been disputed property of man and vermin ...

The weather grew warmer and ... I shared a tent with one of the range riders. Many men went under the canvas every summer, so that an encampment of some fifteen or twenty tents sprang up in the scrub that sheltered some of the buildings.[3]

Walker's memories of riding for the Coldstream Ranch are also useful in providing insights into the daily life of the cowboy at the time. Although he was inexperienced, he had done some riding and was chosen to join the working cowboys instead of being placed in any of the other jobs that the Coldstream had to offer.

In rounding up cattle on the range, a greenhorn invariably got the dirty work—that was part of his initiation. The full-blooded cowboy—the man who had spent a lifetime in perfecting his craft—considered himself among the elite of ranch hands. He had been through the school, yet seldom had the opportunity of bossing others, therefore why should he ride hard after the stragglers that had broken away from the bunch, or flank a herd on a rough hill-side when the valley bottom was smooth and the going easy?

As a greenhorn, I soon found my best friend was my pony. He knew far better than I what a recalcitrant steer meant to do, and if normally clever, thwarted such efforts perfectly. Indeed, given a "cow wise" cayuse, and open country, little remained for the rider to do but stick on. When, however, man and pony were engaged on close work, such as cutting out, roping, etc., the riders' knowledge had to be no less, and every bit as swift in execution as that of his mount, otherwise the twain were soon parted. To expedite this, the methods perfected by riders to guide their mounts were reduced to the greatest simplicity and speed. To the Westerner the reins were not used as a check. To stop, the rider simply threw his weight back in the saddle; to go forward, the reverse. A deviation from the direct course was effected as easily; the swing of the reins meant more to a cayuse than hard pulling on the bit meant to an Old Country hack. Only those who have ridden and worked these clever brutes, can fully appreciate their knowledge of their duties.[4]

A 1907 prospectus for the Douglas Lake Ranch mentions the various sources of labour and their wages at the time. "The class of labour being employed are: white, Indians, Chinese ... the Chinese, who are paid on a lower rate from the Whites. Cowboys are paid at the rate of $25 a month and

Crew in front of the bunkhouse at the KLO Ranch near Kelowna. Every race and nationality was represented at the large ranches in B.C.

their board. Chinese $15 to $20 and the man in charge of the cattle for market, $75 per month. A storekeeper, blacksmith, the Chinese Cook and assistants are continually employed." Another essential employee in a large ranch was a harness and saddle maker. Edwin Godley, who hailed from Booneville, Indiana, came to the Douglas Lake Ranch in 1890 as a harness and saddle maker and was still there 50 years later, faithfully repairing damaged tack and making a wide variety of harnesses and tack.

The cowboys spent most of their waking time in the saddle, but they were also excellent shots with a rifle, a necessary ability in country where predators were a constant threat to the cattle, and they were loyal. For cowboys to "ride for the brand" meant that they would stand by their employers through thick and thin. These attributes would stand them in good stead in the wars that would ravage the new century.

The Bosses

When large corporations such as the Western Canadian Ranching Company, which owned the Gang Ranch as well as land near Kamloops, the British Columbia Cattle Company in the South Okanagan and the Douglas Lake Cattle Company assembled large tracts of land to go into ranching in a big way, the first order of business was to find capable individuals to look after the operation. This presented a challenge, for management of a huge cattle operation required expertise in a wide variety of areas, ranging from accounting to range management. It was soon recognized that one individual could not provide all of these skills on his own and that, as long as the ranch manager understood the basic principles of range management and cattle handling, a cow boss could be hired to look after the cattle on the ranch and a trail boss could be responsible for getting the cattle to market, leaving the manager to focus on the business end of the operation. Each of these positions was essential to the efficient operation of a ranch, and the three had to work together like a person's head, hands and feet. These bosses made sure that the cowboys were cared for and kept on task, making them part of the overall ranch team so that, even in the most trying times, the operation of the ranch ran smoothly and, as much as possible, profitably.

J.B. Greaves

Joseph Blackbourne Greaves (pronounced "graves") was born in Pudsey, Yorkshire, England, in 1831. He received a basic education and trained to be a butcher like his father. At the age of 14, he ran away from home and found a job tending pigs on board a sailing ship bound for America. He arrived in New York City and for the next nine years worked at various jobs across the eastern United States. Energetic and restless, Greaves recognized the potential of the American west, which was opening up after the California gold rush, and travelled overland to California in 1854 where he worked for 10 years. News of the Cariboo gold rush prompted the intrepid Greaves to sink all his earnings into cattle and sheep. He drove them north, sold them at a profit in British Columbia, then returned to Oregon and bought another herd of cattle to drive north. This time, however, he failed to find a market for all of his cattle. He turned the unsold ones loose along the Thompson River west of Kamloops Lake and went to work as a butcher at Soda Creek.

After working for two years for Isaac Van Volkenburgh at Soda Creek, a restless Greaves decided to return to California.

Joseph Blackbourne Greaves, "Old Danger," ruled the Douglas Lake Ranch like a benevolent dictator.

On impulse, he went to see if any of his cattle had survived on the Thompson River. To his amazement, he discovered that not only had they survived, but they also had calves, yearlings and two-year-olds. He immediately branded these "slick-ears" and continued on his way to California. As soon as he arrived there, he came down with a severe fever and spent a few months in a hospital. This "down time" gave him a chance to think about his life and he determined to return to British Columbia and settle down.

Greaves travelled north and searched out his twice-abandoned cattle herd, which by then was becoming sizable and marketable. He decided to stay with it on the north bank of the Thompson below Savona's ferry, and he ranched there for four years without attempting to secure legal title for his land. He finally applied for a pre-emption of 320 acres in 1872, by which time the market for cattle was over in the Cariboo but was growing on the coast. Several times each summer, Greaves would pick out a small group of two- and three-year-old steers and dry cows and hire a few local Shuswap Natives to help him drive them to Cache Creek, then down the Fraser River to Yale or New Westminster. From there, he would send his cowboys home and accompany his cattle by steamboat to Victoria where buyers would welcome him, knowing his reputation for providing excellent beef. The Victoria *British Colonist* made mention of his cattle on two occasions in 1876.

30 April 1876 – Mr. Greaves brought down thirty-one head of fat beeves from Cache Creek.

11 June 1876 – Mr. Greaves of Cache Creek brought in a band of about twenty head of fine cattle for F. Reynolds, by the Enterprise yesterday. We have seen larger cattle but seldom any in better condition.

Johnny Wilson, also from the north of England, had taken up land immediately to the west of Greaves, and the two neighbours became good friends. Greaves cemented the friendship in the mid-1870s when he married 20-year-old Mary Ann, the daughter of Wilson's deceased Lillooet Native wife. Mary Ann, whose natural father, Tom Cavanaugh, had been a gold miner, and Greaves had four children, Joseph, Peter, Alice and Mary.

By 1879, Greaves owned almost 1,000 acres of land but was already looking with interest at the increased activity of the CPR survey crews. Where there were surveys there would soon be construction, and Greaves wanted to be sure to guarantee his share of the lucrative beef market for the crews. To have any hope of winning the beef contracts for the CPR crews he would need capital and lots of it, so Greaves convinced Victoria butcher-shop owner Benjamin

Van Volkenburgh to approach a number of successful businessmen that he knew to raise capital to purchase enough cattle to secure the beef market for CPR construction crews. Van Volkenburgh came through for Greaves and succeeded in amassing the necessary capital.

At the same time, Greaves was working with Charles Miles Beak, who owned about 8,000 acres of land in the Nicola Valley, to enter into a partnership. After some negotiation, Beak agreed to enter into a five-year agreement with Greaves as "farmers and cattle raisers" whereby the two men would work together in the cattle business with the newly formed syndicate of Van Volkenburgh, Ward, Thomas, Pemberton and O'Reilly. This was the final piece in the puzzle that brought about the Douglas Lake Cattle Ranch that Greaves was to manage for the next 25 years.

Greaves's tireless efforts to establish the Douglas Lake Cattle Ranch came with a heavy price. His wife, Mary Ann, and his four children left him and moved to Grande Prairie (later Westwold) in the mid-1880s; and he was forced to sell his own ranch to Johnny Wilson in 1888 when it became too much for him to manage. But, over the years, Douglas Lake Ranch consistently proved itself to be one of the best-operated ranches in the country, and Greaves's reputation flourished.

Greaves continued to look after the purchase of cattle for the ranch well into the 1900s, travelling to the Okanagan every fall to buy cattle. In this sense he was the "banker" for the Okanagan ranchers as far south as Okanagan Mission (present-day Kelowna). He would advance the stockmen money on their cattle in the fall for delivery in the summer. In June, Greaves and his cow boss, Joe Coutlee, would return with 15 to 20 cowboys to collect the cattle, working their way north from the Mission (Kelowna). The outfit travelled light, taking only three pack ponies and a six-by-eight tent. The tent covered the food and Greaves shared it with the cook, but the cowboys, including Joe Coutlee, spread their bedrolls on the ground, rain or shine.

On one occasion, Greaves was at the Thomas Wood Ranch at the foot of Wood Lake gathering cattle to drive north. Mrs. Wood was watching at the corral one day when she saw one of the Native cowboys, nicknamed "Buckskin Joe," spurring his horse's flanks while trying to head off an uncooperative cow. Mrs. Wood, an active member of the Society for the Prevention of Cruelty to Animals, was not impressed and threatened to have the man arrested for cruelty to his horse. Greaves was keen to avoid trouble and agreed to send the man over in the morning so Mrs. Wood could give him a good talking to. However, to avoid any fireworks, Greaves convinced Joe Coutlee to pose as "Buckskin." Coutlee, the son of a French father and

Native mother, was a man with a sense of humour and the courteous charm associated with the French. Coutlee rode to the house and stood politely as Mrs. Wood went up one side of him and down the other. Finally, he promised graciously that it would never happen again and departed, much to the delight of his fellow cowboys.

On another occasion, Greaves was returning from one of his cattle buying trips accompanied by one of his Native cowboys, Jules. It was winter and Greaves had purchased a small flask of good Scotch whisky to warm him on his journey home. As they proceeded along the trail from Merritt to the Douglas Lake, Greaves reached into his sheepskin coat for the flask. Ever mindful of range etiquette, Greaves handed the flask over to his travelling companion to offer him a swig but, in light of the relatively small quantity of whisky, said, "Have a drink, Jules, but just a small one, remember." The loyal Jules took a small swig and passed the flask back to Greaves with a grunt of thanks. They rode on for some time when Jules reined his horse alongside Greaves again and reached into his own winter coat for a large bottle of whisky. Passing it to his boss, he said, "Have a drink, Greaves, but a good big one."

During his time at the Douglas Lake Ranch Greaves earned the nickname "Old Danger," probably in recognition of his stern expectation that every man would pull his own weight. He used to sit at the head of the table in the cook shack like an Old Testament patriarch, ladling great piles of food onto his cowboys' plates, saying, "Go ahead, eat it. If you can't eat, you can't work and if you can't work, you're no good." Nonetheless, he was loved by all his cowboys, who were always prepared to go that extra mile for him, knowing that he would do the same for them.

Greaves maintained regular contact with his wife and family, who still lived at Grande Prairie, one of the Douglas Lake Ranch wintering areas. When his son Joseph Junior came of age, Greaves was happy to offer him a job cowboying at the Douglas Lake Ranch. Joe was a wild young man and, like so many of his fellow cowboys, rather fond of strong drink. On one occasion, Joe was in charge of a branding crew and, when the day's work was done, brought out a supply of liquor to celebrate. At the height of the party Greaves stormed in and erupted in fury at his son's presumption. He fired his son immediately, took the saddle from his horse and ordered him off the range. Joe walked the 15 or so miles to Nicola Lake, borrowed two horses from the Guichons, then rode off to find work elsewhere. Years later, when Joe married, his father bought him the Carieus Ranch for $70,000, saying, "He never asked for anything so there must be good in him." However, Joe Junior soon drank away his ranch and, after his father's death, returned to work at the Douglas Lake Ranch.

In 1910, at the age of 79, Greaves sold his share of the Douglas Lake Ranch to W.C. Ward and retired to Victoria. Before he left, he presented three of his oldest employees, Joe Coutlee, Bob Bearisto and Billy Fountain, his favourite Native cowboy, with purses in recognition of their long service. Fountain also received many of Greaves's personal effects as well as some farm machinery and Greaves's saddle. All who had known him in his 25 years at the Douglas Lake Ranch bid him farewell with great sorrow. In 1915, just five days short of his 84th birthday, he died in Victoria. Most of his staggering $605,932 estate went to charities with only a small amount left to his children.

R.L. Cawston

Richard Lowe Cawston was born on February 10, 1849, in the Stratford area of southern Ontario, where his grandfather and family had settled after leaving Wiltshire, England, in 1825. As a young man, he learned to plow a straight line behind a team of horses, cut grain with a cradle and, in his spare time, swim in the Avon River, a skill that would stand him in good stead in future years. Cawston grew to be a powerful young man, tipping the scales at over 200 pounds in spite of his rather average height of 5 feet 7 inches. He stayed on the family farm until he was 24 years old except for brief stints working as a swamper in a bush camp across the border in Michigan and as a travelling salesman for McColl Brothers.

Cawston arrived in the South Okanagan in 1872 to work for his uncle, William Lowe, who was in partnership with J.C. Haynes in the cattle business in the Osoyoos Lake region. Cawston worked for Lowe for 10 years as his ranch foreman and learned the cattle trade from the ground up. Lowe soon recognized his abilities and made him the first choice to be the "boss driver" on frequent cattle drives over the Dewdney Trail between the South Okanagan and Hope. An early settler in the Similkameen remembered Cawston:

A left-handed crack shot with the rifle, Cawston always maintained that the 1873 Winchester was the best rifle ever made, but he also had a gentle side. Susan Allison, a pioneer in the Princeton area, recalled being woken one night by a gentle tapping at her window. It was Cawston calling her to come outside and witness a glorious display of the northern lights. She sat with Cawston and his cowboys and watched for more than two hours. As she later said, "There was no sound but the awed voices of the men. It was like a glimpse of the 'Beauty of the Lord,' and we all felt it to be such."

Cawston appreciated and cared for the Native cowboys who formed most of the ranch hands in the early days. In 1883, when an epidemic of smallpox raged throughout British Columbia, he received vaccine from the government to vaccinate the Native people of the Similkameen and South

Okanagan valleys. When he realized there was not enough to go around, he was forced to use his initiative. He pushed a number of pins through a whisky bottle cork and stuck each one into the pox sore of someone who was already infected. He then inserted the pin into a healthy arm, transferring the infection and effectively vaccinating the man. The result, while not pretty, had the desired effect. Cawston remarked, "They all took and had arms as big as their legs." The epidemic passed by the area with no casualties.[5] For his efforts, Cawston received $300 from the government, which he promptly invested in a gold watch and chain.

Like many others before him, Cawston worked long enough to be able to afford his own ranch. William Lowe died in 1882, and in 1884 Cawston bought the "R" Ranch in the Lower Similkameen south of Keremeos. In 1885, he travelled to Stratford, Ontario, and returned with a bride, Mary Ann Pearson. Their "honeymoon" trip was from Stratford to Port Huron, Chicago, St. Paul and Spokane by train, then six days on horseback to the Kettle River and on to Osoyoos. Here they spent Christmas with the Haynes family and then rode over the Richter Pass to their new home.

Cawston continued to ranch and was the first choice among the ranchers of the area as trail boss for the numerous cattle drives going east and west on the Dewdney Trail. While the earliest drives were west to Hope and the coastal markets, the 1890s saw regular drives to the new markets in the mining communities of the Kootenays. The trail east involved a difficult crossing of the Columbia River at Trail where the cattle had to be forced into the water and headed straight across the wide river. Cawston developed a unique technique for dealing with problem steers that panicked on entering the water and would not follow the herd across. He would leave his horse on the bank and dive in alongside the steer, pulling its head under water a few times, which usually sent it bawling after the herd.

On one occasion, when the mining excitement was at its peak, two of Cawston's cowboys, Ozzie Coulthard and Charlie Allison, had picked up a few samples of rock from along the trail, hoping to have them assayed. On reaching the Columbia crossing, there was even more confusion and reluctance to enter the water than usual. To make matters worse, a steamboat rounded the bend and her warning whistle scattered the herd. Some of the cattle began to stampede back down the trail, in spite of the whooping and yelling of the cowboys. Cawston, in desperation, grabbed some rocks to throw at the lead animals. As the last rock bounced off its target, he was heard to remark, "Well, there goes Ozzie's gold mine!"

In 1903, Cawston decided to move his family to Ontario so his children could receive a better education. By then, he had a distinguished grey head of hair and a closely clipped beard, giving him a striking resemblance to the new king, Edward VII. The Stratford, Ontario, hockey team happened to be on the same train during one journey, and, as Cawston passed through the day coach, one wit shouted, "Hail to the King!" Much to his delight, Cawston received a standing ovation, applause and cheers that he imperiously acknowledged. Before long the truth of the distinguished gentleman's identity came out and Cawston had the last laugh.

Andrew Stobie

Andrew Stobie was born at Duns in Berwickshire, Scotland, on October 3, 1866, and came to Canada at the age of 21 to take care of the sheep operation for the Western Canadian Ranching Company, who operated the Gang Ranch. After 5 years, he took over the cattle operations of the Gang Ranch as well and for the next 30 years worked as the operations manager.

Andrew Stobie was a true character. Harry Marriott, who worked for him in 1912, described him as "a freckle-faced man with square shoulders and large frame, with light brown hair and sand-coloured moustache."[6] Alexander Gillespie, who was also from Berwickshire, worked for Stobie in 1902 and 1903. He recounted the results of Stobie's attraction to hard liquor.

> The only time he was really annoyed with me was once when he, and an Indian boy and I were over mending some fences on the range across the Chilcotin River. Unfortunately, the Risky [sic] Creek Saloon was not very far away. This Ranch Store and Gin Mill was run by a Mr. Beecher. This attraction was too much for poor old Stobie. He told the Indian boy and myself to keep on patching up the fence and he would ride around and inspect the rest. That evening, no Stobie turned up in camp, nor was he there the next morning, so I decided I would go over to Risky Creek and see if he was there—and of course he was, sure enough.
>
> He had been very cunning, as he had ridden over on the old packhorse "Buckskin," whom he knew would take him back to camp, as long as he could stay in the saddle, no matter how drunk he was. I managed to persuade him to mount Buckskin and we started for camp. About half way there, Stobie said he was feeling sick and wanted to get off and lie down. He told me to tie up Buckskin and go on back to camp, which I did. The Indian boy and I had our supper and expected any moment to see Stobie come riding in. It got dark and still he didn't come, so I decided he had gone back to Risky Creek and went to bed.
>
> Somewhere in the small hours of the morning, I was nearly frightened out of my wits by the very irate Stobie grabbing and shaking me violently,

swearing like a real cowboy and wanting to know why the ___ I hadn't tied up that ___ Buckskin. I had tied up Buckskin, but that little horse knew that if you keep on pulling at a knot with your teeth, it sometimes comes undone and this one did. Some packhorses know as much as men.[7]

Lord Strathcona's Horse

Donald Smith was an apprentice clerk for the HBC who, through hard work and perseverance, worked his way through the ranks to become the company's chief executive officer and eventually its major shareholder. He was the chief financial backer for and an enthusiastic supporter of the CPR and was invited to drive in the last spike when the railway was completed in 1885. In 1896, Smith was appointed Canadian High Commissioner in London and became active in British political affairs. The following year he was made a British peer and took the name Lord Strathcona.

Lord Strathcona strongly supported Canada's role in the British Commonwealth, and when Britain became embroiled in the South African War, he offered to raise and equip a mounted regiment in Canada at his own expense. The regiment, named Strathcona's Horse, was to consist of three squadrons, one to be raised in Manitoba, one in the Northwest Territories (present-day Alberta and Saskatchewan) and one in British Columbia. Commanded by Superintendent Sam Steele of the North West Mounted Police, Strathcona's Horse was recruited from the Mounted Police and from the ranches of western Canada. The response was overwhelming. Steele even received an offer from 600 Arizona stockmen who were willing to supply their own arms, horses and equipment. But, as he noted, "Recruits were not wanting; one could have got thousands of the best men in Canada."[8]

By early February 1900, recruiting was complete. The ranching community of British Columbia was well represented with Kamloops and the Okanagan Valley contributing a large number of experienced horsemen, mostly hard-riding cowboys. On March 18, 537 officers and men and 599 horses sailed from Halifax. The regiment arrived in Cape Town after a rough sea voyage that took the lives of 120 horses. After taking some time to adjust to the climate and terrain of South Africa, the troops were ordered to proceed up the east coast by boat and then inland to blow up a bridge and cut the Boer communication lines. Unfortunately the Boers learned of the plans, the mission was cancelled and the regiment was withdrawn to Durban.

The Strathconas joined the Third Mounted Brigade in Natal on June 20 and took part in General Buller's pursuit of the Boers into the Transvaal. The tenacity, stamina and initiative of the rugged westerners were ideal

The Vernon contingent of Lord Strathcona's Horse shortly after recruitment. This mounted regiment attracted many cowboys, who were lured by the promise of adventure and travel.

British Columbia members of Lord Strathcona's Horse. The X marks William Brent, the mixed-blood son of Fred Brent, who operated the first gristmill in the Okanagan.

to combat the Afrikaners' unorthodox guerrilla tactics. Because of these qualities and their superb horsemanship, the Strathconas were made scouts for the advancing army and were often the first to make contact with the enemy, resulting in dozens of casualties.

Twelve members of Strathcona's Horse lost their lives in action in South Africa. One of the first was Edmond Parker of the Kootenays, who was killed near Waterval Bridge. Parker was a member of a troop sent out in response to an offer of surrender by a group of Boers. As the troop cautiously advanced they were attacked and Parker, being on the flank, came under heavy fire. The Boers called upon Parker to surrender but he shouted back at them defiantly, whereupon he was shot and wounded. He was picked up by a farmer and kept in a house until medical attention arrived, but he succumbed to his injuries before he could be moved.

Private William Henry Ingram, son of the original settler at Grande Prairie (now Westwold), was the last Strathcona to be killed in action. On December 23, 1900, he and Corporal Macdonnell were sent to cover a *kopje* (ridge) near Clocolan, at some distance from the main force. When they reached the top, they came face to face with eight Boers who had come up the other side. They dismounted and opened fire with their revolvers; the Boers returned fire with their rifles. Three of the enemy were killed and two wounded. Ingram was killed and Macdonnell was also shot through the torso, but walked four miles to Clocolan. The Irish Yeomanry, who fought alongside the Strathconas, sent a wreath for Ingram's grave when he was buried.

Initially the British cavalry looked upon the Strathconas with some amusement because they all rode western saddles and carried lassos, part of the standard issue that Sam Steele had insisted upon. However, the ropes proved to be invaluable in capturing wild horses on the veldt and in dragging others out of bogs or sloughs—the ex-cowboys were masters at throwing a loop over the head of bogged horses and pulling them to safety. Perhaps the best demonstration of their cowboy skills came at Paardekop, where a band of 500 fresh horses from Natal broke out of a *kraal* (Afrikaner for corral) and galloped off across the veldt. With whoops of glee the Strathconas grabbed their ropes and rode after them, succeeding in lassoing half of them. The remainder were rounded up and driven back to the corral. In return for their cowboy services, which could not have been accomplished without lassos and stock saddles, they were given the pick of the remounts. From then on, the British maintained a healthy respect for these cowboys from "the colonies."

In January of 1901, the regiment received word that it was to be recalled to Canada. The men were delighted to learn that they were to return via London.

They arrived in London on February 14 and their patron, Lord Strathcona, greeted them for the first time. They received a royal welcome and received their medals from King Edward VII in person. Edward, who had not yet been crowned following the death of his mother, Queen Victoria, also presented the regiment with a King's Colour, a unique honour for mounted units of the British Empire. The regiment was wined and dined in London and went out to the theatre every night, something the simple cowboys found a distinct contrast from their usual lifestyle at home.

The regiment arrived back in Halifax on March 8, and the men returned home to the west. Enthusiastic crowds greeted them at every station stop and special celebrations were held in their hometowns. Not only had they shown the hardiness and resolve of Western Canadian fighting men, they had also helped to establish the unique value of Canada as a country within the British Commonwealth.

Wild Horses: The Thrill of the Chase

During the early years of the twentieth century, British Columbia experienced tremendous population growth, and newcomers to the province moved into all the areas that could possibly be used for farming. The increasing number of farms and ranches sparked a demand for horses, and prices reflected the growing value for good stock. For many of the young cowboys, the wild horses found in the remote areas of the interior looked like easy money to be made during slack time at the ranches. The horses were considered fair game, and as long as they did not carry anyone's brand, they were "slick ears," a name more properly referring to calves with no earmark or brand. However, it was not a task for an amateur. Catching wild horses in the rough backcountry required a sure-footed saddle horse, knowledge of the terrain and a combination of determination and luck.

The South Okanagan was home to large bands of wild horses. As early as 1833, David Douglas had referred to the "River of Wild Horses" in the South Okanagan. He probably meant the Marron River as the term "marron" comes from the French meaning "feral." Wild horses roamed the area from Marron Lake past Eneas Lake on both sides of the valley. The country provided excellent bunchgrass range as well as watering holes and salt licks for them. Many of them were fine horses, descended from stock that had escaped from immigrants or local ranches. Hundreds of wild horses lived at Kruger Mountain in the years before the First World War.

At Tule Lake on Kruger Mountain, there was a huge corral built from good-sized logs with wings extending half a mile in each direction to funnel the horses into the corral. Springtime, just after the snow had melted, was the accepted time for wild-horse roundups before the tough little animals recovered their strength after pawing through snow for their feed all winter. Mounted on sure-footed cow ponies that had been well fed all winter, the cowboys tried to run the wild horses into the large log corral.

Another band of horses lived on Wild Horse Mountain, which is a range of hills between Kaleden and Marron Valley. It was headed by a light bay stallion, with a black tail and mane, that lorded it over 10 or 12 mares. Experienced riders from all over the district tried to catch this stallion without success. Whether he was in a log corral or ropes, he managed to escape every time.

Wild horses also abounded east of the Okanagan Valley along the Dewdney Trail in the Kettle Valley. The McMynn family ranched in the Midway area and frequently hunted wild horses. One particular band was led by an escaped stallion that, unlike the small, stocky wild horses, stood 16 hands high and weighed about 1,200 pounds. He was a dark bay with a white spot on his forehead, which earned him the name Star. Every attempt to corral this magnificent stallion had failed. Each summer, Billy and Jim

Horse roundup in the South Okanagan. Wild horses were found in abundance in the wooded mountains of the Okanagan.

McMynn organized a horse hunt and, on one occasion, managed to corral Star, whose vision was so obscured by dust that he did not see the corral. He was trapped along with about 200 head of wild horses. The McMynns offered 20 head of horses to anyone who could break the stallion, so Arthur "Cowboy" Kean and his brother, Albert, drove him into a small corral. There they forefooted him and tumbled him to tie him down then saddle him. Arthur Kean mounted him and went for the ride of his life. The stallion bucked and reared and turned his head to try and bite Kean's feet, but he stayed on, with his brother herding the horse to keep him from hitting the corral fence. That first ride lasted about an hour and a half before the exhausted horse and rider called it quits. Several months later the stallion was fully broken and turned out to be a superb saddle horse. Kean told the story in the *Star Weekly* some years later.[9]

Countless wild horses inhabited the Chilcotin as well, especially on the ranges north of the Chilcotin River. Alexander Gillespie recalled a wild horse roundup in the spring of 1903 when a Mr. Hawden of Duncan purchased 250 head from the Gang Ranch, to be rounded up and delivered to Ashcroft.[10] Hawden confidently expected to find a market for the scrubby wild horses in Toronto, so the Gang Ranch agreed to come up with them.

All the Chilcotin Natives in the neighbourhood participated in the hunt with the local ranchers, all expecting to make a few dollars for their efforts. The drive began at daylight because the horses were in the open then, usually seeking the protection of the timber during daylight hours to avoid flies and predators. A large group of cowboys under the leadership of an experienced hand would surround one of the small open valleys common in that country where there would be one or two bands of horses feeding. The surrounding had to be done with the utmost caution, as the mere breaking of a branch would send the spooky horses into the timber where it would be impossible to move them. Cowboys were placed at the head of the trails into the timber to turn back the horses into the open valley bottom when the main group of men appeared at one end of the valley. Then the chase would begin, with everyone riding at a full gallop as the wild horses were headed out into an open area where they could be surrounded and held until they settled down enough to be manageable. The whole herd would be driven off towards a huge figure-eight-shaped log corral where they could be sorted out, with the branded horses either being taken away by their owners or turned out to range again. The wild, unbranded "slick ears" were run into the adjoining corral and held there.

The hunt for wild horses lasted for nearly a month, and when the required number of horses was obtained, they had to be driven to Ashcroft.

The cowboys assigned to the drive had their hands full, especially on the first day which involved crossing the Chilcotin River. At first, the horses refused to enter the water and began to mill, threatening to stampede. Eventually the lead mares were headed into the river and the rest followed. At night, the horses were put into a corral if one was available. This meant that they did not have a chance to feed, so the next morning they had to be driven slowly to let them feed and water at any lake or stream. After a few days, the horses settled into the routine and were relatively easy to handle as they kept together and did not try to break away.

The drive proceeded down the Cariboo Road for 10 days, encountering freight wagons and pack trains along the way. The horses churned up thick dust that covered horses and riders alike with a uniform coating. At Ashcroft the horses were put into stock corrals and then run up a chute into the cattle cars. Fifteen carloads of horses left Ashcroft and headed east under the careful eye of Mr. Hawden and a few cowboys who stayed to handle the horses at the end of the railway trip. As it turned out, Hawden decided to sell them in Calgary and received a good price for them from Alberta ranchers hungry for good mounts. The cowboys who had stayed with him from the beginning received the sum of $90 for their efforts.

Alexander Gillespie accompanied the horses all the way to Calgary, after which he was hired by Fisher Williams, who ran a livery stable at Olds, to return to British Columbia to help him buy more horses from the Alkali Lake Ranch. The Alkali had been established in 1861 by Herman Otto Bowe and was one of the first ranches in British Columbia. Gillespie travelled by train back to Ashcroft then headed north to Alkali Lake. By then, Bowe had turned over the operation of the ranch to his son, John. The same mad dash after wild horses ensued, except that this time the horses were stronger after a spring of good feeding, making it much more difficult to catch them. Fortunately fewer horses were required than the last time, and before long the hunt was over. Gillespie recorded that the cowboys celebrated the successful horse hunt with a classic old-time country dance:

> On the last day, by way of celebration, a dance was held in the old Bowe house. It was attended by all the youth and beauty of the district, with all the girls in most colourful calico dresses. I think every girl was either a half or quarter breed and mostly quite pretty. The men all wore the regulation cowboy outfit with high heel boots and coloured handkerchiefs round their necks. The music was fiddle and an old piano, which was declared to have come over the old Cariboo Road by pack horses. The dances were the old Minuet and square dances, with a man calling off the figures. At supper, the

men all sat down and the ladies waited on us. It was most amusing and was kept up till the sun was well up the next morning.[11]

The Chinese Cowboys

Chinese workers arrived in British Columbia in the earliest years of the gold rush and travelled to every mining area. They became well known for taking over claims that were considered to be worked out and, through fastidious mining practices, making the claims pay good wages. When they were not directly involved in mining, the Chinese would often work as labourers for the large mining companies that needed ditches to carry water into areas for hydraulic mining. In fact, many of the Chinese were brought into British Columbia by large companies that hired them out to the highest bidder until they had worked off the cost of their travel to North America. The same applied during the construction of the CPR, when thousands of Chinese were brought into the province by contractors who received a percentage of their wages in return for bringing them in.

When the railway construction was completed in 1885, many of the Chinese settled in British Columbia and looked for meaningful employment. During the late 1800s and early 1900s many of the ranches in British Columbia employed Chinese labourers during haying and harvesting and for irrigating. As well, Chinese were frequently hired as cooks on the roundup outfits. Eventually these cooks proved to be capable and hard-working enough to be hired on by the large ranchers to cook for the home ranch. The records of the O'Keefe Ranch back into the 1890s show Chinese cooks in charge of preparing meals for the family and cowboys alike, and the Chinese cooks' bunkhouse still stands on the ranch.

The Chinese rarely worked on horseback, but a handful of Chinese ranch workers graduated to the job of cowboy and proved as indispensable at herding cattle as they were at cooking or general agricultural tasks. One of these was Kin Nauie, who worked for years for the family of Alexander Graham who had arrived in the Chilcotin in 1887. Graham's C1 Ranch at Alexis Creek was a going concern when Kin Nauie arrived in 1903. He had crossed the Fraser River in a canoe a few miles from where the Chimney Creek Bridge was later located and walked all the way to Alexis Creek looking for work. He found a job with Graham and spent the next 30 years working for the Graham family. Graham's daughter, Kathleen Telford, later described life in the remote Chilcotin in the early years of the 1900s: "While the men were away on these tedious cattle drives and freighting trips to Ashcroft, the women, children and hired hands kept the ranches going. The hired hands were usually Chinese and every large rancher employed one. They were loyal and efficient, working hard at jobs such as irrigating hayfields, milking cows, repairing ditches and flumes, and similar ranch chores. Our hired hand, Kin Nauie, remained with dad from 1903 to 1934 then returned to China."[12]

During branding and fall cattle roundup and the occasional wild-horse roundup, Kin Nauie would join the other cowboys on horseback and hold his own in the excitement and chaos of the chase. He also regularly assisted in moving cattle from summer to winter pasture and back in the spring. On one occasion, he was helping Graham push cattle across the Chilcotin River in sub-zero fall weather. Conditions were treacherous and ice was forming on the rocks, Constable Robert Piper of the Provincial Police was helping the cowboys drive the cattle into the freezing Chilcotin when his horse slipped and went under. Graham threw Piper a rope, and he and his horse made it to shore, but Piper's prize Stetson went floating off down the river. No slouch with a rope, Kin Nauie neatly lassoed the hat and brought it safely to shore.

After 30 years with the Graham family Kin Nauie returned to his family in China. But he missed the life on the ranches and returned to the Chilcotin two years later. Learning that his former boss, Alex Graham, had died, he hired on with Duke Martin at the old Graham Ranch and stayed for nearly 20 more years.

Sin Tooie was another Chinese who successful adapted to ranch life. Born in 1890, he was 20 years old when he left his home in Canton, China, and sailed to Canada to look for work. He took the train from Vancouver to Ashcroft and then headed for the Chilcotin. He was lucky enough to find a freight wagon headed for Hanceville that he could travel north with. As he later recounted, "I go with Indian freight wagon. We walked and walked and camped and camped. It rained. God damn it rained. We roll in blanket at night. No tent, no can get dry."[13] It took 17 long days to reach Hanceville via the Gang Ranch. There he went to work for Alex Graham, no doubt at the urging of his countryman, Kin Nauie. He was a hard-working ranch hand, able to do anything asked of him, and later proudly recalled, "I cowboy, I work on irrigation ditches, I learn to cook, I mend machinery, I plough, I do any damn thing." He earned $30 a month and worked 10 hours a day. After saving his wages for two years, he returned to China and married then returned to Graham's. By 1930 he was a cowboy at the Chilco Ranch and could rope and tie a calf with the best of them. But because of his versatility, he was still doing "any damn thing." He cooked for as many as 27 men, mended mowing machinery, cut logs, butchered beef and rode out looking for strays. During his stay in the Chilcotin he returned to China five times and fathered two sons and two daughters, none of whom were allowed to come to Canada due to the discriminatory immigration laws in place at the time. He eventually owned his own café in Williams Lake.

Not all Chinese were relegated to the labour end of the ranching business. Some succeeded enough in other ventures to be able to purchase land and become ranchers. One example is Tong Sing, known to all by the name Joe Duck, who made enough money operating a store at Cache Creek to purchase a ranch in the Upper Hat Creek area. By the turn of the century he was running close to 2,000 head of cattle on his lands and growing timothy and clover crops for feed. In 1907, the recently widowed Mrs. Kwan Yee took up a homestead to the south of the Duck Ranch. Kwan Yee moved in with Joe Duck a few years later, and her sons joined the working cowboys of the Duck Ranch. The Kwan boys looked after the cattle all winter, and their supply of excellent hay guaranteed that they would have fat cattle for sale all through the winter months. After the death of Kwan Yee in 1912, the sons continued to cowboy on the Duck Ranch but eventually left to further their education.

The Next Railway Frenzy

The new century heralded a frenzy of railway construction in British Columbia under Premier Richard McBride's government. In 1903, owners of the Grand Trunk, the oldest railway line in Canada, announced plans to extend the line to the Pacific coast. After considerable negotiation and various charges of corruption, the government announced early in 1908 that the Grand Trunk Pacific Railway would be constructed in British Columbia from the Yellowhead Pass through Fort George to terminate at Prince Rupert. The same year, the Canadian Northern Railway Company announced that it would construct a line running from the Yellowhead Pass down the North Thompson River to Kamloops and then paralleling the CPR to Vancouver. Then, in 1910, the CPR announced that it would construct a branch line, the Kettle River Valley Railway from Hope to Midway. Later, in 1912, the Pacific Great Eastern Railway Company announced that it would construct a line from North Vancouver via Squamish and Lillooet to Quesnel. This railway would unite North Vancouver with the Grand Trunk Pacific Railway at Fort George, providing Cariboo-Chilcotin ranchers with easy access to the coastal markets. All of these railways would need huge work crews to complete the work on time, and the crews would have to be fed. The ranchers of the B.C. interior were in a perfect position to supply cattle to all of these markets.

Pat Burns, the great butcher/entrepreneur, secured the contract to supply beef to the Grand Trunk Pacific, some stretches of the Canadian Northern Railway, the Kettle River Valley Railway and the Pacific Great Eastern construction camps in British Columbia. He bought up all the cattle he could and prices rocketed as the market struggled to keep abreast of the demand for beef to supply the railroad builders. Providing beef to the Grand Trunk Pacific proved to be a particular challenge. Construction in British Columbia began from both ends at once, from Prince Rupert in the west and from the Yellowhead Pass in the east. Most of the cattle for the west end of the line could be sent by the CPR from Alberta or the southern interior to Vancouver and then by scow to Prince Rupert and up the Skeena River to the camps, but reaching the construction camps along the Fraser River in the Rocky Mountain Trench was more difficult. Cattle purchased in the Cariboo were loaded on scows and shipped upstream along the Fraser River to the construction camps. For much of the big bend in the Fraser after Fort George the going was smooth and easy, but after the bend the river proceeded between steep banks through a series of rapids. These culminated in the Grand Canyon of the Fraser, where the cattle had to be unloaded and driven overland while the scows were pulled through the churning rapids. By 1910, the line was complete to the new railway town of Prince George and construction began from both ends to connect Prince George to Hazelton. For this stretch of road, cattle had to be driven overland from the Cariboo-Chilcotin to Hazelton. The drive was through brush, mostly red willow, so the cattle had to be strung out single file and the going was slow.

In the spring of 1910, Burns and Company agents began to purchase large herds of cattle from all over the Cariboo and Chilcotin areas and assemble them at Riske Creek. Old-time cowboy Joe Payne, who was working full-time for Burns and Company at the time, led the first trail drive. From Riske Creek the cattle were driven to the west side of the river at Quesnel and then 500 miles along the old overland telegraph trail to Hazelton. When this drive proved successful, more drives were sent north regularly all summer long. Recruitment of cowboys to work on these drives took place in Kamloops. Some of the cowboys who signed up at Kamloops included Ulysses Campbell, who was foreman on the second and many subsequent drives, Antoine Allen, Wes and Bill Jasper, Johnny Cannon, Gus McGregor, Ezra Knapp, Abe Spooner, Alva Shaffer, Jack Laidlaw and Pete Duncan. The crew assembled at Ashcroft and received saddles and packhorses from Cy Hyman, another old-time cowboy who was working for Pat Burns. The crew travelled north to Canoe Creek and then to Chezacut in the Chilcotin where the roundup began. Most ranchers in the Chilcotin did not feed their cattle in winter at that time, and the cattle were therefore wild. Cy Hyman had already arranged to purchase most of the cattle, at about $50 a head for three-year-old steers, $60 for anything older and $35 for cows. From Chezacut, the cowboys trailed the cattle south, picking up more cattle at the ranches along the way until they reached Riske Creek with about 800 head. Riske Creek remained the main assembly point for the herds heading north for the next four years.

At Riske Creek, the cowboys branded all the cattle with Burns's trail brand of NL and shod the saddle horses before the herd was ready to drive north. In early May, the first group of 500 head of cattle were headed north with the remaining 300 forming the nucleus of the next drive to leave 30 days later. Seven cowboys, a cook, a packer/horse wrangler and about 45 horses herded the cattle. For the first few nights, the cattle had to be night-herded, with two riders taking each shift, changing one at a time every two hours. The cowboys followed the west side of the Fraser River for eight days until they reached Quesnel. From there, they picked up the old telegraph trail through the bush. The narrow trail meant, of course, that the cattle had to be strung out in single file with each cowboy falling in every 50 head. He remained in that position until the day's drive was over unless help was needed getting the lead cattle across a mud-hole or boggy creek.

The cowboys fell into a daily routine of counting the cattle out in the morning, riding all day, counting the cattle at night and living on the usual fare of bacon, beans, bannock and coffee. The cattle slowly made their way up the telegraph trail until they reached Fort Fraser before they were rested for a couple of days and then swum across the Nechako River. To make this crossing easier, the crew constructed a pole corral and chute and two of the cowboys crossed the river on an old wooden scow to hold the cattle on the other side. Two Natives with canoes were hired to point the leaders across, and after waiting two hours so that the sun did not shine in the cattle's eyes and obscure their view of the far bank, the cattle were pushed into the river and across without a problem. At Fort Fraser, a beef was butchered and used as trade for supplies, with the balance being used up for a gallon of Hudson's Bay rum, which was greatly appreciated by the cowboys.

The drive reached the Hazelton area where the cattle were driven, as required, to the Burns and Company slaughterhouse that supplied the construction camps. Two cowboys were left to herd the cattle, and the remaining cowboys, leaving their saddle horses behind to be sold, returned by rail to Prince Rupert, boat to Vancouver and rail to Ashcroft. There they picked up a supply of fresh horses to ride to the Chilcotin and start the process all over again. During that summer three more drives of 500 head arrived at Hazelton, making a total of about 2,000 head of cattle that were driven to Hazelton. As winter approached, additional drives were made so that by November 1, Burns and Company could butcher and freeze about a thousand carcasses to last until the first drive in the spring arrived.

During the next three years, another 10,000 head of cattle were purchased and driven to the Grand Trunk Pacific construction crews. As the grass along the old telegraph trail became grazed off from the constant flow of cattle, a drive led by Harry Curtis tried a new route north from Alexis Creek via the Nazko River where they found excellent bunchgrass sidehills. The route followed an old Native trail that crossed the Blackwater River and Mud River and joined the telegraph trail about three days north of Fraser Lake. By 1912, the railway contractors had constructed a wagon road west from Burns Lake and driving cattle was much easier. As supplies of cattle dwindled in the Cariboo and Chilcotin, Burns and Company shipped Alberta cattle as far as Kamloops where they could be fed and wintered before being driven to the various railway construction camps. The final big drive, consisting of 860 head of cattle driven by 15 cowboys, left Riske Creek on November 10 and arrived at Fort George on December 5. Since 1910, about 12,000 head of cattle had been driven to the Grand Trunk Pacific Railway crews. Every rancher in the Cariboo-Chilcotin had been given a boost, and the cattle industry had become well established.

Unfortunately, construction of the Pacific Great Eastern Railway was tainted with charges of corruption and poor management. By the time the track was laid from Squamish to Clinton in 1917, the entire appropriation of $20 million had been spent. By the early 1920s the line only reached to Quesnel, and no one could be convinced to buy the struggling railway.

Horses of a Different Colour

There is something about the freedom that comes with living on the frontier away from the structures of civilization that attracts characters that would never fit in anywhere else. These men or women can truly be said to "march to the beat of a different drummer." In a frontier society composed of so many different nationalities and cultures, tolerance was the order of the day and a person's eccentricities were generally accepted as long as they did not hurt his neighbours. If a man chose to live as a hermit away from all human contact, or if he simply refused to wash his face, the society of the time accepted him for what he was: another human being trying his best to cope with the cards he had been dealt. This tolerance meant that some peculiar characters were drawn to the frontier, and the British Columbia ranching community had more than its fair share.

Cowboy at Hazelton. The six-shooter is probably an addition, there being no need for a handgun on the long drives north.

Coutts Marjoribanks: Mud Pup Extraordinaire

One of the truly colourful characters in the Okanagan Valley in the 1890s was Coutts Marjoribanks (pronounced "march-banks"). The younger son of the aristocratic Marjoribanks family, Coutts was educated in the best British schools but showed no inclination to pursue an academic career. In fact, Coutts Marjoribanks had a boisterous and outgoing nature and a decided tendency to outdoor activity. Although the aristocratic upper class could indulge their love of the outdoors in the socially acceptable joy of the chase, this did not seem to be enough for Coutts. His family decided when he was still very young that he was destined "for the colonies" to join the other overly energetic younger sons of England's best families who had gone before him. So it was that, in the mid-1880s, Coutts was placed in the care of the owners of the Horse-shoe Ranch in North Dakota (the United States was considered a step below but part of the Empire nonetheless). The western ranching way of life was just what he needed to bring him into his own. He took to cowboying like a duck to water, and relished the rough and ready lifestyle that sneered at the more placid approaches to accomplishing things. His skills in riding, roping and handling cattle grew, but his family regarded his lifestyle as far from acceptable. As his niece, Lady Pentland, put it, "Coutts was not prospering there."

The answer to the dilemma that Coutts posed to his family seemed near at hand. His older sister, Ishbel Maria Marjoribanks, had married Lord Aberdeen and so become Lady Aberdeen. Lord and Lady Aberdeen, enthralled by the Canadian west, particularly the Okanagan Valley, purchased the 13,261-acre Coldstream Ranch near Vernon in 1891. To the Marjoribanks family it seemed opportune, as there was one family member with experience in looking after a large ranch: Coutts Marjoribanks. History has recorded that Lady Aberdeen was the dominant partner in her marriage, and in this case as in many others, her will prevailed. Coutts was installed as the manager of the Coldstream Ranch.

Coutts Marjoribanks's tenure at the Coldstream was not a happy one—at least not for the owners. He really preferred the daily activities of cowboying to the paperwork of management. His true love was the cowboy lifestyle, which he lived with all the passion and recklessness he could muster. The famous Canadian poet Charles Mair described Coutts in a letter written from the Okanagan in 1892: "Lord Aberdeen's large ranches are here, looked after

Coutts Marjoribanks (seated) and his foreman at the Horse-shoe Ranch in North Dakota. Coutts took to the cowboy way of life like a duck to water, but "was not prospering there."

by his brother-in-law, Marjoribanks—a rum stick who goes about dressed like a cowboy, and indulges freely in Scotch whisky. Not a bad chap though with all his horseplay, and antics."[14] Like most who met Coutts during this time, however, Mair could not resist his flamboyant personality and admitted begrudgingly to liking the character.

When Coutts first arrived at the Coldstream, one of the local wags insisted on pronouncing his surname as "major-eye-banks" with the accent on the middle syllable. This was soon shortened to "Major" and before too long the stories of Major's exploits became legend in the Okanagan. He was notorious for riding his horse into the Kalamalka Hotel bar when he wanted a drink, which was whenever he was in town. To his credit, this would have involved some good riding, as the steps to the hotel were steep. General opinion was that "his riding excelled his management of the ranch."[15] In later years, C.W. Holliday, who had lived in Vernon at the time, described him:

> A big burley man, always wearing a cowboy hat and usually mounted on his big black horse "Cap," he liked to ride into town at a clattering gallop to pull up short in front of the Kalamalka Hotel where he would dismount for a refresher … On one occasion the ranch was shipping a bunch of cattle by train, and I was sitting on the high timber fence watching the cattle milling about beneath me. A little way along the fence sat the Major who was directing the operations, and on his other side sat Mr. Langill, the Presbyterian minister. The Major was giving his instructions with the usual lurid language suitable to the occasion when the parson, with a mistaken sense of duty, had to butt in. "Really, Mr. Marjoribanks," he said, "don't you think that a man in your position should be showing a better example to the men in your employment?"
>
> "Hell, man!" exploded the Major, "I'm not teaching a Sunday school, I'm loading cattle, and I'm giving the boys the best example I can. And I'll bet that Noah swore when he was loading his animals into the ark."[16]

A clue to Coutts's alternative managerial behaviour lies in the Vernon Police Court Record for 1894. Charged with being "disorderly and throwing stones," he pleaded guilty and was fined $10 and costs, plus $2.50 for damages, presumably to replace the windows that got in the way of his stones. It was soon evident to all concerned, and particularly to his sister, Lady Aberdeen, that Coutts was not cut out for managerial duties. In 1895, he "resigned" as manager of the Coldstream but stayed in the area, purchasing property and building a house. Living close to the ranch, he could always join in on the roundups and the other activities that were most dear to his heart.

The Big Kid

By the 1890s, the clothing and gear of the cowboy were becoming universally recognizable and almost predictable. Most cowboys sported a wide-brimmed hat and high-heeled boots, usually complemented by a bandana around the neck and a set of spurs jingling on the heels. But the Big Kid broke all the rules. If ever there was a cowboy who didn't look like a cowboy, it was him.

Jim Madden appeared in the Nicola Valley during the 1890s and, judging by the thick Scottish burr in his speech, must have originated from the Scottish Highlands or Hebrides Islands. When in his cups he was known to mutter about great catches of fish, which led one to believe that he had been a fisherman in his earlier days. But, true to the unwritten code of the ranching country, no one ever asked about his past, and he seemed to prefer it that way. His exuberant personality and childish innocence soon resulted in his being everywhere known by the nickname "The Big Kid," for such he was. The simplicity of his lifestyle and his colourful adventures soon made him legendary in the Nicola and surrounding valleys.

He was a large man, over six feet in height and a full-bodied 240 pounds. In size and sheer physical presence, he was everything that a cowboy dreamed of being. But the resemblance to the typical cowhand stopped there. His shaggy hair was shoulder length and seemed to continue via his long beard to his woolly chest, creating one continuous mat of hair. His clothing was equally distinct, with his only concession to standard dress being an ancient flop-brimmed hat, stained and worn with the sweat and dirt of many days' hard work. The rest of his attire consisted of a plaid wool shirt and heavy wool pants stuffed into a pair of lace-up boots. Even in the most frigid weather, his clothes remained unchanged. Only the degree to which the shirt and boots were done up, ranging from wide open in the height of summer to fully closed in winter's coldest months gave any hint that the changing of the seasons affected him at all.

During his time in the Nicola Valley, the Big Kid lived in two different cabins. The first and more permanent of these, referred to as "The Boar's Nest" for reasons that any visitor would find obvious, was on the Douglas Lake Ranch alongside a field that is still known as the Boar's Nest. The Big Kid's building techniques were as unique as his appearance. He selected building logs for their proximity to his cabin site rather than their straightness. This resulted in a series of large holes between the logs that were too large to fill with the conventional mud and straw chinking. But the Big Kid was undeterred. He collected a variety of empty liquor bottles from behind the local watering hole, the Quilchena Hotel, and used them to fill the largest holes. This successfully filled the cracks and also allowed daylight in without the need for windows. The end result created an interior like that of a medieval cathedral with sunlight filtering through stained-glass windows.

An independent spirit, the Big Kid chose to work by contract for the ranches in the area. During roundup and branding, he could ride and rope with the best of them, but he most often chose jobs that he could perform on his own, preferring to live alone. Fencing, land clearing, wood cutting and occasionally winter feeding numbered among his favourite tasks. It was while putting up a log fence for the Douglas Lake Ranch that the Big Kid found himself in a jam that any other man might have considered disastrous. The logs were pine and oozing with pitch from the hot spring weather. As the Big Kid worked alone, he had to wrestle the logs into place and soon found the work hot and sweaty. He had to remove his shirt and open his woolly chest to the spring air to keep cool. But, as the pitch in the logs began to accumulate on his chest, he found that eventually his beard became glued in place, keeping his head in a permanently stooped position. Undeterred, he continued the job until, at the end of the day, he appeared at the ranch headquarters with his beard welded to his chest. It took the extensive application of kerosene and the careful manipulation of horse clippers for the Big Kid to manage to tilt his head far enough back to take a drink directly from a bottle.

The Boar's Nest remained the Big Kid's bachelor home for many years and, like many bachelors, his dietary preferences and sanitary standards were often dubious at best. Most often, boiled beans or boiled whole wheat were both the main course and dessert, but more exciting fare could occasionally made its way onto his rude table. Such was the case on the day the local minister, showing a zeal for visiting the poor and needy, chose to drop by the Boar's Nest. The Big Kid's welcome was genuinely warm and friendly. He extended an invitation to the reverend to stay for lunch, which, the man of the cloth could see, consisted of a pot of beans boiling on the stove. The minister, undeterred by the fact that the Big Kid's shirt was off and his furry chest exposed, readily agreed. As they exchanged news and discussed their views on local events, the Big Kid explained that he was suffering from a cold he could not shake. In the course of conversation he seemed to be paying extremely close attention to a chunk of pork fat that was boiling along with the beans. He checked it regularly to see if it was done, and sometime before lunchtime, he fished it out of the pot and plunked it on his plate. The minister was struck by the particular attention that the Big Kid was paying to this chunk of pork. From time to time, he would touch it gently and turn it over carefully. Finally, at what he must have deemed the right moment, he seized the chunk and, explaining the beneficial properties of hot pork grease, rubbed it all over his massive hairy chest. Then, much to the minister's surprise, he carefully dropped the chunk back into the bean pot to reheat for lunch. History does not record the minister's reaction to this versatile chunk of pork in his lunch, but, mindful of the obvious hospitality extended to him, he proceeded to eat lunch, watching carefully for curly chest hairs in his teeth.

The Big Kid built his second cabin when he was working on an extended contract clearing a field along Quilchena Creek for the Triangle Ranch. The field is known to this day as the Big Kid Field, in many ways a monument to this industrious and colourful character. Somewhere around the turn of the century, the Big Kid spent a winter in this cabin and suffered severely frostbitten toes. The locals puzzled over how a man could suffer frostbite while sleeping in his own cabin, but the explanation eventually came to light. It seemed that the Big Kid was not lavish in his sleeping arrangements. He preferred to crawl between two cow hides rather than waste his hard-earned money on wool blankets. Apparently, during a particularly bitter winter night, the cow hides, not known for their square dimensions, slipped out of place. The Big Kid, preferring to keep his head warm as opposed to his feet, left his feet uncovered and the result was disastrous.

This cabin was also the setting for another of the Big Kid's gourmet escapades. Once again, a visitor had dropped by and had been generously invited for lunch. The Big Kid hinted that there was something special cooking on the stove, but the visitor felt somewhat dismayed when he spotted a long black tail, which bore a suspicious resemblance to that of a muskrat, protruding from the pot. Sure enough, when lunchtime arrived, the Big Kid pulled from the pot a muskrat complete with hide, guts, feet and eyes. Then, before the visitor's astonished eyes, he stripped the skin off and placed the cooked carcass on a plate. Carefully spooning out wheat that had been boiled in the same pot, he dug in with relish. Once again, we have no record of the visitor's reaction, but we can assume that he hardly did justice to this lunchtime feast.

The Big Kid spent the years around the First World War as a hand at the Guichon Ranch, still preferring to live alone in his own log cabin. By that time he had accumulated enough worldly possessions to fill a cowhide trunk, but despite his impoverished appearance, the Big Kid was far from broke. He once complained to Lawrence Guichon about losing $600 in cash. The Big Kid was a supporter of the Red Cross and had recently been badgering Guichon to donate. Guichon got the Kid to promise that if he could find the money, 10 percent of it would go to the Red Cross. Sure enough, Guichon found it under an old cup without a handle lying upside down on the floor of the Big Kid's cabin. True to his word, the Big Kid donated $60 to this worthwhile cause.

The Big Kid stayed in the Nicola Valley for close to 30 years, living in semi-retirement at the Guichon Ranch into the 1920s. But, sad to say, his story does not end happily. Toward the end of his days, a long-lost brother showed up and convinced him to invest his life savings in a sawmill near Princeton, B.C. The sawmill venture failed and the Big Kid lost everything. According to rumour he died in the Prince George area and is buried near there.

Val Haynes—The Last of the Old-Time Cowboys

Valentine Carmichael Haynes, the eldest child of J.C. Haynes and his wife, Emily Pittendrigh, was the quintessential cowboy. He was born on December 21, 1875, in the midst of a snowstorm and was delivered by a Native mid-wife, Mrs. McDougall, from Colville. By the time he was eight years old, he was cowboying with the best of the hands on his father's large ranch in the South Okanagan. After the death of his father in 1888, the family returned to Emily's home in England, where Haynes completed his education.

But ranching was in his blood, and when he returned to Canada in 1893, he went to work for Tom Ellis, who had acquired the vast Haynes family holdings and whose ranch headquarters were at present-day Penticton. When the Shatford brothers bought out Tom Ellis in 1905, Val became the foreman for the ranch and worked for them until they sold to the government in 1919.

Valentine Carmichael Haynes. It can safely be said that Val was the last of the old-time cowboys in the Okanagan.

Haynes rapidly gained a reputation as a cowboy among cowboys. His abilities were outstanding, and even though he never showed much interest in rodeos or competition, he was considered the best in roping in difficult places and under adverse conditions. He prided himself on his knowledge of cattle and often remarked that "I know all my cattle by the look on their faces." Despite being an excellent horseman, Haynes was never too fond of horses, knowing that the South Okanagan was home to thousands of wild horses that consumed large quantities of the precious bunchgrass resource, leaving less for his beloved cattle. In appearance he was every inch a cowboy with his large, flat-brimmed Stetson, silk neckerchief and woolly chaps.

Val Haynes branding a calf. Haynes is applying his distinctive "69" brand to the calf's right hip, a brand originally used by Tom Ellis of Penticton.

During his time in Penticton, Haynes was out riding after cattle near dawn on a cold winter day between Christmas and New Year's when he noticed the tracks of five men in the snow. Following the tracks, he found one man after another frozen to death in the snow. Finally he came across the fifth man, who had just fallen and was lying near death. Haynes picked him up and dressed him in his coat and gloves, then pulled off his thin patent leather shoes and carried him on his horse to Summerland. The man, who survived, was one of five blacks who were on their way to serve New Year's dinner in Summerland. The tragedy always puzzled Haynes, who remarked that the weather wasn't really cold and the snow had even started melting. Unlike Haynes, however, who was known to sleep out in any weather with just the shirt on his back and a saddle blanket, the men were unaccustomed to the cold and could not survive in winter temperatures dressed as they were.

Val Haynes acquired the Garrison Ranch and range and later the Swan Lake (Vaseux) Ranch and the range on Kruger Mountain. He married Elizabeth Runnels, whose mother was sister of Nespelem George, one of the most respected Native chiefs of the northwest. Haynes became one of the most respected ranchers in the Okanagan, never failing to help out one of the old-time cowboys, whether White or Native, if he needed a hand. In all his years as a foreman and rancher, he always ate at the same table as his hired men and always referred to them as his cowboys, never his hired men. He was an excellent judge of cattle and horses and built his ranch up to be one of the finest in the province. His stock was always considered the best, and he never had to sell through the cattle auctions at Okanagan Falls—he shipped directly to the buyers and commanded top price.

Considered the last of the old-time cowboys, Haynes remained an active cowboy until a month before his death. It had been his habit for years to wean the calves on December 14, and on December 21, his birthday, he would drive the calves to Swan Lake Ranch. His last birthday, his 87th, was no exception, and with the help of his grandsons he drove some 200 calves about 20 miles. It can safely be said that his death in 1962 marked the end of an era in the history of ranching in British Columbia, an era that saw the lowly drover capture the attention of the world and be transformed in the eyes of all who saw him into a figure of mythological proportions: the cowboy.

ENDNOTES

Introduction

1. Reinhart, *The Golden Frontier: The Recollections of Herman Francis Reinhart 1851–1869*, p. 129.
2. I have used the American spelling of Okanogan for the river and the fort south of the forty-ninth parallel.
3. Oliphant, *On the Cattle Ranges of the Oregon Country*, p. 10.
4. Ibid.
5. William Manson, "Fort Kamloops Journal," January 1859 to November 1862, Kamloops Museum and Archives.
6. Mayne, *Four Years in British Columbia and Vancouver Island*, p. 301

Chapter One: The Drovers

1. *Oregon Argus*, July 3, 1858.
2. *Portland Democratic Standard*, July 1, 1858.
3. *Oregon Statesman*, February 14, 1860.
4. "Contributions to the Historical Society of Montana," Volume II.
5. *The Oregonian*, January 28, 1860.
6. *British Colonist*, quoting the *Portland Times*, March 2, 1861.
7. Sir James Douglas to "the Gold Commissioner of Shimilcomeen" (J.C. Haynes), Colonial Correspondence, May 19, 1862.
8. Haynes to Young, Colonial Correspondence, June 10, 1864.
9. William Lowe to Colonial Secretary, Colonial Correspondence, August 26, 1866.
10. William George Cox to W.A.G. Young, Colonial Secretary, Colonial Correspondence, March 3, 1861, Provincial Archives of British Columbia.
11. Hills, "Diary," July 10, 1862, Anglican Provincial Synod of British Columbia Archives.
12. J.C. Haynes to Young, Colonial Correspondence, August 31, 1863.
13. Milton and Cheadle, *North-West Passage by Land 1865*, p. 225.
14. Mayne, *Four Years in British Columbia and Vancouver Island*, p. 296.
15. Splawn, *Ka-mi-akin, the last hero of the Yakimas*, p. 164.
16. Ibid.
17. Ibid., p. 168.
18. Frost, "Account of 1858 Journey with David McLoughlin."
19. McInnes, "Dunlevy's Discovery of Gold on the Horsefly."

20. Diaries of Myron R. Brown.

Chapter Two: The Ranchers
1. Weir, "Ranching in the Southern Interior Plateau of British Columbia."
2. Quoted in "From Gypsy Boy to Cattle King" by P.W. Luce, *Canadian Cattlemen*, February 1951.
3. *British Columbian*, December 9, 1863.
4. *Cariboo Sentinel*, June 24, 1865.
5. *British Colonist*, December 10, 1874.
6. *Ashcroft Journal*, February 9, 1939.
7. Eric D. Sismey, "Joseph Richter," *Thirty-Fourth Report of the Okanagan Historical Society (OHS)*, 1970, p. 13.
8. Ibid.
9. Eliza Jane Swalwell, "Girlhood Days in Okanagan," *Eighth Report of the OHS*, 1939, p. 36.
10. Ibid., p. 34.
11. Ibid., p. 36.
12. Maria Brent, "The Indians of the Okanagan Valley," *Sixth Report of the OHS*, 1935, p. 122.
13. Sydney Russell Almond, "History of the Kettle Valley District," *Tenth Report of the Boundary Historical Society*, 1985, p. 35.
14. Holliday, *The Valley of Youth*, p. 176.
15. Richard J. Loudon, "An Odyssey: The Loudon Family in Retrospect," memoir in the possession of Jean Barman and quoted by her in "Lost Okanagan: In Search of the First Settler Families," *Okanagan History—Sixtieth Report of the OHS*, p. 8.
16. Gowan, *Church Work in British Columbia*, p. 20.
17. Frank B. Ward to Brian Kesteven de Peyster Chance, quoted in Woolliams, *Cattle Ranch: The Story of the Douglas Lake Cattle Company*, p. 157.
18. *British Colonist*, June 28, 1872.
19. Henry Nicholson, *Fifth Report of the OHS*, 1931, excerpted from the *Hedley Gazette* and *Similkameen Advertiser*, January 10, 1905, p. 30.
20. British Columbia Archives, GR-0868.
21. Dawson, *The Journals of George M. Dawson: British Columbia*, p. 318.
22. McDougall, *Opening the Great West: Experiences of a Missionary in 1875-76*, p. 26.
23. John Bunn to Richard Hardisty, August 14, 1875, Hardisty Papers, Glenbow Archives.
24. McDougall, *Opening the Great West*, p. 37.
25. *British Colonist*, April 20, 1876.
26. *British Colonist*, May 21, 1876.
27. *British Colonist*, February 5, 1878.
28. *Inland Sentinel*, Yale, April 7, 1881.
29. *Inland Sentinel*, Kamloops, November 27, 1884.

30. Dorothy Hewlett Gellatly, "The Chinook Jargon," *Tenth Report of the OHS*, 1943, p. 125.

31. Ibid.

32. Sismey, "Joseph Richter," p. 15.

Chapter Three: The Rise of the Cowboy

1. *Nanaimo Free Press* and *British Columbian*, April 19, 1882.

2. *Inland Sentinel*, Kamloops, January 28, 1886.

3. F.M. Buckland, "From Ranches to Orchards," *Twelfth Report of the Okanagan Historical Society (OHS)*, 1948, p. 97.

4. *Vernon News*, January 12, 1893.

5. "Suppliers of Beef to Dawson," *Canadian Cattlemen*, 3: 1, June 1940.

6. Mora, *Trail Dust and Saddle Leather*, p. 13.

7. Frank Newstand to Brian Kesteven de Peyster Chance, Kamloops Museum and Archives.

Chapter Four: The Open Range Era

1. Allison, *A Pioneer Gentlewoman in British Columbia: Recollections of Susan Allison*, p. 66.

2. Holliday, *The Valley of Youth*, p. 191.

3. Allison, *A Pioneer Gentlewoman*, p. 54.

4. *Vernon News*, February 1894.

5. John Ruskin, quoted in *Heaven's Command: An Imperial Progress* by James Morris, p. 318.

6. Harker, "The Bayliffe Story."

7. Lee, *Klondike Cattle Drive: The Journal of Norman Lee*.

8. Marriott, *Cariboo Cowboy*, p. 30.

9. *Inland Sentinel*, Yale, April 7, 1881.

10. W.R. Carruthers, "Edward Maurice Carruthers, J.P.," *Thirty-Second Report of the Okanagan Historical Society (OHS)*, 1968, p. 107.

11. E.M. Carruthers, "Stories of Early Days—Told to W.R. Carruthers," *Forty-Fourth Report of the OHS*, 1980, p. 64.

12. *Inland Sentinel*, Kamloops, November 25, 1886.

Chapter Five: The Changing Face of Ranching

1. Marriott, *Cariboo Cowboy*, p. 29.

2. Gillespie, "Journey Through Life," p. 17.

3. B. Eyre-Walker, *Rolling On: The Log of a Land Rover*, p. 20.

4. Ibid., p. 24.

5. Verna B. Cawston with Gint Cawston, "The First R.L. Cawston (1849–1923)," *Twelfth Report of the OHS*, 1948, p. 127.

6. Marriott, *Cariboo Cowboy*, p. 17.

7. Gillespie, "Journey Through Life," p. 25.

8. Steele, *Forty Years in Canada*, p. 340.

9. A.D. Kean, "Star," *Toronto Star Weekly*, April 16, 1932.

10. Gillespie, "Journey Through Life," p. 18.

11. Ibid., p. 24.

12. Kathleen A. Telford, "Pioneer Days in the Chilcotin," from *Pioneer Days in British Columbia, Volume 3*, Art Downs, ed., p. 13.

13. Stangoe, *History and Happenings in the Cariboo-Chilcotin*, p. 57.

14. Letter by Charles Mair, August 23, 1892, quoted in the *Forty-Second Report of the OHS*, 1978, p. 60.

15. Grace Worth, "Autobiography (1900-1910)," *Thirty-Third Report of the OHS*, 1969, p. 113.

16. Holliday, *Valley of Youth*, p. 184.

REFERENCES

Published Sources

Allison, Susan. *A Pioneer Gentlewoman in British Columbia: Recollections of Susan Allison*. Margaret Ormsby, ed. Vancouver, BC: UBC Press, 1976.

Bulman, T. Alex. *Kamloops Cattleman*. Sidney, BC: Gray's Publishing Ltd., 1972.

Dawson, George Mercer. *The Journals of George M. Dawson: British Columbia*. Two volumes. Douglas Cole and Bradley Lockner, eds. Vancouver, BC: University of British Columbia Press, 1989.

Downs, Art, ed. *Pioneer Days in British Columbia. Volumes One through Four*. Surrey, BC: Heritage House, 1973, 1975, 1977, 1979.

Drumheller, Dan. *"Uncle Dan" Drumheller Tells Thrills of Western Trails in 1854*. Spokane, WA: Inland-American Printing Co., 1925.

Lee, Norman. *Klondike Cattle Drive: The Journal of Norman Lee*. Surrey, BC: TouchWood Editions, 2005.

Eyre-Walker, B. *Rolling On: The Log of a Land Rover*. London: Seeley, Service & Co. Ltd., n.d.

Frost, Robert. "Account of 1858 Journey with David McLoughlin." Written in 1901 and quoted in *Washington Historical Quarterly* XXIII (1931): p. 204.

Gowan, Herbert H. *Church Work in British Columbia, Being a Memoir of the Episcopate of Acton Windeyer Sillitoe, D.D., D.C.L., First Bishop of New Westminster*. London: Longmans, Green and Co., 1899.

Harris, Lorraine. *Halfway to the Goldfields: A History of Lillooet*. Vancouver, BC: J.J. Douglas Ltd., 1977.

Holliday, C.W. *The Valley of Youth*. Caldwell, ID: Caxton Printers, 1948.

Jordan, Terry G. *North American Cattle-Ranching Frontiers: Origins, Diffusion and Differentiation*. Albuquerque, NM: University of New Mexico Press, 1993.

Laing, F.W. 1942. "Some Pioneers of the Cattle Industry." *The British Columbia Historical Quarterly*, 6: 4, October, 1942.

Marriott, Harry. *Cariboo Cowboy*. Surrey, BC: Heritage House, 1994.

Mayne, R.C. "Report on a Journey in British Columbia in the Districts Bordering on the Thompson, Fraser and Harrison Rivers." *Journal of the Royal Geographical Society* #31, 1861.

———. *Four Years in British Columbia and Vancouver Island*. London: John Murray, 1862.

McDougall, John. *Opening the Great West: Experiences of a Missionary in 1875–76.* H.A. Dempsey, ed. Calgary, Alberta: Glenbow–Alberta Institute, 1970.

McInnes, Alexander P. "Dunlevy's Discovery of Gold on the Horsefly." *Chronicles of the Cariboo.* Lillooet, BC: Lillooet Publishers, 1938.

Milton, Viscount and Dr. W.B. Cheadle. *North-West Passage by Land 1865.* Coles Canadian Collection. Toronto, ON: Coles Publishing, 1970.

Mora, Jo. *Trail Dust and Saddle Leather.* Lincoln, NE: University of Nebraska Press, 1987.

Morris, James. *Heaven's Command: An Imperial Progress.* London: Faber and Faber Ltd., 1973.

Oliphant, J. Orin. *On the Cattle Ranges of the Oregon Country.* Seattle, WA: University of Washington Press, 1968.

Patenaude, Branwen. *Trails to Gold, Volume One.* Victoria, BC: Horsdal & Schubart, 1995.

———. *Trails to Gold, Volume Two: Roadhouses of the Cariboo.* Surrey, BC: Heritage House, 1996.

Reinhart, Herman Francis. *The Golden Frontier: The Recollections of Herman Francis Reinhart 1851-1869.* Doyce B. Nunis Jr., ed.. Austin, TX: University of Texas Press, 1962.

Splawn, A.J. *Ka-mi-akin, the last hero of the Yakimas.* Portland, OR: Kilham Stationery & Printing Co, 1917.

Stangoe, Irene. *History and Happenings in the Cariboo–Chilcotin.* Surrey, BC: Heritage House, 2000.

Steele, Samuel Benfield. *Forty Years in Canada: Reminiscences of the great North-West with some account of his service in South Africa.* New York, NY: Dodd, Mead, 1915.

Van Arsdol, Ted. "Trail North: 1858." *Okanogan County Heritage*, March and June (1969).

Weir, Thomas. "Ranching in the Southern Interior Plateau of British Columbia." Department of Mines and Technical Surveys. Ottawa, ON: Queen's Printer, 1964.

Woolliams, Nina G. *Cattle Ranch: The Story of the Douglas Lake Cattle Company.* Vancouver, BC: Douglas & McIntyre, 1985.

Archival Sources

"Contributions to the Historical Society of Montana," Volume II (1896). Historical Society of Montana, Helena, MT.

Gillespie, Alexander. "Journey Through Life." Unpublished autobiography. MS-1649, Provincial Archives of British Columbia, Victoria, BC.

Glenbow Archives, Calgary, AB.

Harker, Douglas E. "The Bayliffe Story." Typescript. 1987. MS-2528, Provincial Archives of British Columbia, Victoria, BC.

Hills, Bishop George. "Diary." July 10, 1862. Anglican Provincial Synod of British Columbia Archives, Vancouver, BC.

Kelowna Museum, Kelowna, BC.

Letter from Frank Newstand to Brian Kesteven de Peyster Chance. Kamloops Museum and Archives, Kamloops, BC.

Manson, William. "Fort Kamloops Journal January 1859 to November 1862." Kamloops Museum and Archives, Kamloops, BC.

Nicola Valley Archives, Merritt, BC.

Palmer, Joel. "Diary of Joel Palmer." MSS 114, Oregon Historical Society, Portland, OR.

Penticton Museum and Archives, Penticton, BC.

Colonial Correspondence. Provincial Archives of British Columbia, Victoria, BC.

Brown, Myron R. "Diaries of Myron R. Brown." Washington State Library, Olympia, WA.

Newspapers and Periodicals

Ashcroft Journal

British Colonist, Victoria, BC

British Columbian, New Westminster, BC

Canadian Cattlemen, Winnipeg, MB

Cariboo Sentinel, Barkerville, BC

Inland Sentinel, Yale and Kamloops, BC

Nanaimo Free Press

Oregon Argus, Oregon City, OR

Oregon Statesman, Salem, OR

Portland Democratic Standard

Reports of the Boundary Historical Society, Grand Forks, BC

Reports of the Okanagan Historical Society, Vernon, BC

The Oregonian, Portland, OR

Toronto Star Weekly

Vernon News

INDEX

Photo Credits

B.C. Archives: pp. 31 (A-03504), 33 (A-01337), 35 (A-02246), 39 (A-03787), 48 (A-00348), 58-59 (A-03661), 61 (B-00937), 72 (G-08010), 119 (A-03771), 162 (A-01652), 175 (G-09139)

Historic O'Keefe Ranch: pp. 11, 29, 65, 122-23, 151

Kamloops Museum: pp. 36-37, 57, 98-99, 102, 124, 158-59, 160

Kelowna Museum: pp. 91, 96, 97, 125, 156-57, 168, 174, 197

Lower Similkameen Indian Band: p. 130

McCord Museum: p. 50 (I-69930.1)

National Archives of Canada: pp. 14-15 (C-088931), 27 (C-071205), 52 (C-88910 top; C-088910 bottom), 68-69 (PA-186457), 94-95 (PA-40901), 126 (PA-186341), 170-71 (PA-020412), 195 (PA-096066).

Old Photos: pp. 74, 79, 132

Oregon Historical Society: p. 18 (OrHi 66086)

Penticton Museum: pp. 29, 31, 54-55, 75, 83, 104-05, 113, 136-37, 146, 164-65, 186, 202-03, 204

Public domain: pp. 40 (*Ben Snipes—Northwest Cattle King*), 41 (*Ka-mi-akin, the last hero of the Yakimas*)

R.A. Moon, Williams Lake: p. 152

Vernon Museum: pp. 128, 142-43, 172 (top and bottom), 183 (top and bottom)

Washington State Historical Society: pp. 20 (Fort Wal 14) and (from Alfred Downing Album) 21, 22, 24

Ken Mather has been involved in researching, writing and interpreting western Canadian heritage for the past 33 years. He started out as a researcher for Fort Edmonton Park in 1973 and left in 1976 to work as a consultant for various heritage and natural history parks in Alberta. In 1979 he moved to British Columbia to become the interpretation and education coordinator at Barkerville Historic Park; he became curator in 1982. From 1984 until 2004 he was the manager/curator of the Historic O'Keefe Ranch near Vernon, where he developed his love of early cowboy history. He was general  manager of the Interior Provincial Exhibition from 2004 to 2006. Ken has written extensively about B.C. ranching history and is a frequent public speaker on a variety of topics. He and his family live on a small farm near Armstrong, B.C.